MW00985687

SIMON&
GARFUNKEL'S
BOOKENDS

SIMON&
GARFUNKEL'S
BOOKENDS

PETE FORNATALE

RODALE

Notice

Mention of specific companies, organizations, or authorities in this book does not imply endorsement by the author or publisher, nor does mention of specific companies, organizations, or authorities imply that they endorse this book, its author, or the publisher. Internet addresses and telephone numbers given in this book were accurate at the time it went to press.

© 2007 by Pete Fornatale, Sr.

All rights reserved. No part of this publication may be reproduced or transmitted in any form or by any means, electronic or mechanical, including photocopying, recording, or any other information storage and retrieval system, without the written permission of the publisher.

Rodale books may be purchased for business or promotional use or for special sales. For information, please write to:
Special Markets Department, Rodale Inc., 733 Third Avenue, New York, NY 10017

Printed in the United States of America
Rodale Inc. makes every effort to use acid-free ♾, recycled paper ♻.

Book design by Drew Frantzen

Library of Congress Cataloging-in-Publication Data

Fornatale, Peter.
    Simon and Garfunkel's Bookends / Pete Fornatale.
        p.   cm.
    ISBN-13 978–1–59486–427–8   hardcover
    ISBN-10 1–59486–427–6   hardcover
    1. Simon and Garfunkel. Bookends.   I. Title.
ML421.S53F67 2007
782.42166092'2—dc22   2007024859

Distributed to the trade by Holtzbrinck Publishers

2   4   6   8   10   9   7   5   3   1   hardcover

We inspire and enable people to improve their lives and the world around them

For more of our products visit **rodalestore.com** or call 800-848-4735

To the memory of my friend
Steve Sawyer

"Until We Meet Again"

CONTENTS

INTRODUCTION

When I first heard their names, I thought they must be lawyers or accountants. I was in my car, listening to an AM radio station in the fall of 1965, when the disc jockey came on and said something like "Here's our Good Guy Pick of the Week—'The Sound of Silence,' by Simon and Garfunkel." The impact was powerful and palpable. The production was very much in the folk-rock style pioneered by the Byrds and Bob Dylan. The song was instantly memorable: "Hello, darkness, my old friend." These two were clearly different. The blend of their voices was pretty, almost angelic, but the message of the song was dark and mysterious and hypnotic. And the language was different too—clever, intricate, and literate. This was intelligent rock and roll!

As someone who thought the Beatles was a stupid

name, I had learned my lesson well: Never judge a book by its cover, and never, ever judge a rock-and-roll group by its name. In a recent history of Columbia Records, it is said that Goddard Lieberson, the esteemed president of the label at that time, is the one who convinced Art and Paul to use their real names for recording. (On previous projects, they had adopted a variety of stage names, such as Paul Landis and Artie Garf.) A couple of years later, when I joined the American Federation of Television and Radio Artists, the membership director tried to persuade me to adopt a more "radio friendly" name. He even suggested a few: "Pete Peters," "Peter Noel," and "Peter Fortune." I distinctly remember thinking about Simon and Garfunkel and deciding to keep my real name, as well. Thanks, guys!

Over the next few years, Simon and Garfunkel singlehandedly (or should I say double-handedly?) raised the IQ of rock and roll by about 10 points. "The Sound of Silence" was just the tip of the iceberg. The duo followed that with a truly exceptional and exhilarating body of work. They immediately assumed a commanding role in the great American rock revolution of the 1960s. Shoulder to shoulder with their peers—Bob Dylan, Roger McGuinn of the Byrds, Brian Wilson of the Beach Boys, John Phillips of the Mamas and the Papas, John Sebastian of the Lovin' Spoonful, et al.—they restored to American rock some of the luster that had been hijacked by the Beatles and the British Invasion.

By the time their third album, *Parsley, Sage, Rosemary and Thyme*, was released, it was absolutely clear that Simon and Garfunkel had ambitions that went way beyond the conventional notion of pop stardom. They had ideas. They had vision. And, most important of all, they had the talent to back them up. It appeared that their aim was nothing less than to stretch the outer limits of contemporary popular music. And they did. Their catalog of songs and albums has already withstood an impressive test of time. It is as appealing to those discovering it today as it was to the audience that embraced it more than 40 years ago. It hasn't been that easy, though, for Simon and Garfunkel to embrace each other. Their complicated partnership truly is one of the most volatile love–hate relationships in music history. But even at their most dysfunctional, they are still capable of resolving their differences and reminding the world of what Simon and Garfunkel was like, at least once in every decade since the sixties. I, for one, believe that, as they sang in "Old Friends," they *will* share that park bench when they are 70!

Looking at the catalog of recordings by Simon and Garfunkel is like looking at a prism. Turn it slightly this way or that and you'll see (and in this case hear) another facet of their talent. Our focus in these pages will be to examine Art and Paul's contribution to the maturation of rock and roll, as well as their role in elevating the art of the "concept album."

Which leads us to a very interesting question . . .

1

"DADDY, WHAT'S A CONCEPT ALBUM?"

What was the first record you ever bought? Was it a 78 rpm, a 45 rpm, a 33⅓ LP, a reel-to-reel tape, an eight-track cartridge, a cassette tape, a compact disc, or (fanfare, please!) a file downloaded from the Internet? How you answer this question connects you to a very specific time frame in the evolution of recorded sound in the 20th century.

Men and women have been making music since pre-historic times. Banging a bone on a hollow log was music. Grunting rhythmically while hunting or working in a field was music. Playing with the echo in a cave was music. Of course, the only ones who heard this "music" were those who were making it and others who happened to be within earshot.

Now let's jump forward a few centuries to a time when more-sophisticated humans took the idea of music to a whole other level. Songs, melodies, and rudimentary instruments sprang up simultaneously all over the globe. Music began to be recognized as a hobby, a diversion, a way to kill time, entertainment, and, finally, an art unto itself.

Music began to be used for specific practical functions: worshipping, celebrating, mourning, preparing for and waging war, expressing love, soothing children, and simply amusing family, friends, and strangers. And so it went until 1877, when Thomas Alva Edison devised a machine—the phonograph—that actually captured the sounds of voices and music and could play them back over and over again—anytime, anyplace.

That was it! That was the sea change: Music became a unifying social force, not just locally but, eventually, globally, with commonality of message available worldwide at the mere flip of a switch or turn of a dial. What was so different about this new means of disseminating music? As Langdon Winner, a political scientist who studies how technology affects social and political issues, beautifully expressed it in his essay about the 1967 release of the Beatles' *Sgt. Pepper's Lonely Hearts Club Band*:

The closest Western civilization has come to unity since the Congress of Vienna in 1815 was the week the *Sgt. Pepper* album was released. In every city in Europe and America, the stereo systems and radios played [the title song] and everyone listened.

———

At the time, I happened to be driving across country on Interstate 80. In each city where I stopped . . . the melodies wafted in from some far-off transistor radio or portable hi-fi. It was the most amazing thing I've ever heard. For a brief while, the irreparably fragmented consciousness of the West was reunified, at least in the minds of the young. Every person listened to the record, pondered it, and discussed it with friends. While it is no doubt true that I have little in common with the gas station attendant in Cheyenne, Wyoming, we were able to come together to talk about the meaning of "A Day in the Life" during those few moments in which the oil in my VW was being changed.

That is why the *Sgt. Pepper* album, *Pet Sounds* by the Beach Boys, and *Bookends* by Simon and Garfunkel were and are so important. As we moved into the 20th century, modifications improved upon Edison's rudimentary phonograph. In response to this burgeoning technology, new industries developed to capitalize on all the opportunities it created. Foremost among them were the record companies; RCA Victor, Capitol, Columbia, Decca, Mercury, and MGM led the pack.

Initially, a disc with a single song on only one side was the norm. Then, songs were placed on both sides of the disc. In the days when only 78 rpm recordings were made, some enterprising marketer came up with the idea of combining several of these discs into a single package called an *album*. Then in 1948, Columbia Records introduced the first 12-inch, 33⅓ rpm, microgroove long-playing album (*LP* for short). This meant that recorded pieces from longer-form performance categories became available on a single disc or a collection of discs. The ways to hear, remember, replay, absorb, and relate to all kinds of musical performances reached new heights of dizzying ecstasy!

Early on, LPs were collections of isolated, unrelated songs by an individual artist, group, band, or orchestra. It didn't take long for someone to figure out that a performer who had achieved a healthy number of mainstream, radio-friendly hit recordings could gather those songs on a single album and call it the performer's *Greatest Hits*. Technically, you could call these best-of collections *concept albums* by default. This formula took off like wildfire and continues in one form or another to this day.

Other early collections of music could also be loosely described as concept albums even if they weren't consciously intended to be. Basically, any album that is unified by a distinctive theme of any kind can be considered conceptual. Early examples include *Dust Bowl Ballads* by Woody Guthrie, from 1940 and *The Lure of the Grand Canyon* by Johnny Cash, from 1961, and, even before he released his masterpiece, *Pet Sounds*, in 1966 (which Paul McCartney has acknowledged was his main inspiration for *Sgt. Pepper's Lonely Hearts Club Band*), Brian Wilson demonstrated his genius and affinity for the form with at least two early Beach Boys albums that were centered around a specific subject, theme, or mood. *Little Deuce Coupe*, released in 1963, contained a dozen pop songs about America's fascination with car culture, and the *Beach Boys' Party!*, from 1965, attempted to loosen up the formality of a studio recording by re-creating the ambience of a teen or young adult party, complete with ashtrays, drink glasses, and off-key singing by some of the guests.

Some of our more ambitious, talented, and visionary musical artists realized early on that you could do a lot more with a long-playing album than collect random musical selections. The more adventurous among them began to write, design, and organize serious song cycles based on a single theme.

A CONCEPT ALBUM?
WHAT A CONCEPT!

In addition to the albums of concerts, symphonies, greatest hits, and subject-related songs already mentioned, two other progenitors of the concept album in popular music have to be acknowledged. One is a category and the other an individual. The category is Christmas albums, of which there are hundreds, and the individual is Frank

Sinatra, one of the towering figures of 20th-century American popular music.

―――――

Sinatra's relationship with rock and roll might best be described as uneasy. Despite his 1957 diatribe declaring rock music to be something performed and consumed by "cretinous goons," Ol' Blue Eyes still deserves credit for his role in the development and popularization of thematically conceptual albums. After his "bobby-soxer idol" status screeched to a halt in the late forties, Sinatra pulled off one of the biggest comebacks in the history of show business. He resurrected his recording career after signing with Capitol Records in 1953 and released a steady stream of artistically, commercially, and critically successful LPs. The distinguishing characteristic of these remarkable recordings was the thematic unity of their content, which showcased every aspect and nuance of the singer's deep reservoir of talent. When Sinatra died in May 1998, *New York Times* critic Stephen Holden wrote of this period:

> Only five years earlier, the long-playing record had been introduced, and the longer form encouraged Sinatra, who brought remarkable introspective depth to the interpretation of lyrics, to make cohesive album-length emotional statements . . . Sinatra's Capitol albums were among the first so-called con-

cept albums in the way they explored different adult approaches to love and invoked varied aspects of the singer's personality.

On the lighter, upbeat side were Sinatra's recordings, such as *Come Dance With Me!* (1959) and *Come Fly With Me* (1958), whose titles alone reveal the interweaving subject matter of the song selections. *Songs for Swingin' Lovers!* (1956) and *A Swingin' Affair!* (1957) defined Sinatra's "Rat Pack" image as a fun-loving, jet-setting playboy. But the LP that solidified Sinatra's credentials as a master of the concept-album form was released in the spring of 1955. Called *In the Wee Small Hours*, the songs chronicled the disintegration and dissolution of his marriage to the ravishing American film actress Ava Gardner, particularly "In the Wee Small Hours of the Morning," "Mood Indigo," "Glad to Be Unhappy," "I Get Along Without You Very Well," "When Your Lover Has Gone," and "I'll Never Be the Same." Unlike most of the great rock-era concept LPs, whose songs were written and sung by their primary composers, Sinatra didn't *write* these songs, but he was an interpreter par excellence. Other equally powerful albums that followed in its wake, such as *No One Cares* (1959) and *Frank Sinatra Sings for Only the Lonely* (1958), only reinforced Sinatra's description of himself as a "saloon singer"—the guy who walks into the bar in the literal wee small hours of the morning.

By the mid-1960s, the foundation was firmly in place

for a new generation of artists, composers, and musicians to expand and develop the still-untapped possibilities of the concept album in a rock-and-roll framework. The first wave of young adults raised on this music had matured without preconceptions about its limitations. In fact, quite the opposite was true. The best and brightest of this new breed felt that the opportunities for artistic expression in the medium were limitless. The image of a rock suggests rigidity, but the rock in rock and roll was, in fact, very flexible and adaptable.

Many of the accepted conventions of songwriting and record making were ignored or abandoned by the cutting-edge rock musicians of the mid-1960s. Dumbing it down was replaced by smartening it up. For one brief, shining moment, it appeared that the influence of artistic considerations would outpace that of commerce in the recording industry. There could be blues rock and folk rock and country rock and jazz rock and even classical rock and rock opera. But the powerful one-two-three punch that made the phrase *concept album* an indelible part of the rock lexicon was those three albums released in 1966, 1967, and 1968: *Pet Sounds*, *Sgt. Pepper's Lonely Hearts Club Band*, and *Bookends*.

We've already mentioned Brian Wilson's early dabbling with thematic recordings, but *Pet Sounds* took everyone (including his bandmates) by surprise. It had the earmarks that one expected from a Beach Boys album—exquisite, tight vocal harmonies; catchy hooks and choruses; adventurous musical arrangements—but this one had something else as well. It had maturity. It had vulnerability. It had the razor's-edge wisdom of a tortured genius grappling with life issues of much greater import than surfing, cars, and girls on the beach. Working with lyricist Tony Asher, Brian explored the thin line that separates adolescence from young adulthood with candor, beauty, and wistfulness. The Beatles had begun to prove it, but *Pet Sounds* made it official and undeniable: Rock and roll had grown up and become a very credible form of artistic expression in the 20th century.

There is probably no greater testament to the impact and influence of *Pet Sounds* than the profound effect it had on Wilson's peers. Countless musicians at the time and right up to this very day point to that album as the one that inspired their own creativity. Of all the honors and accolades bestowed upon *Pet Sounds*, perhaps the greatest and longest-lasting measure of Wilson's achievement is the magnitude of its influence on one fellow musician in particular who, coincidentally, had been born two days earlier than and a continent away from Wilson in June 1942. That musician was James Paul McCartney, who has been steadfast in his praise of Brian Wilson and *Pet Sounds* and very candid and generous in describing how it influenced and inspired his own group's next ambitious long-form project—the standard by which all future rock concept albums would be measured—*Sgt. Pepper's Lonely Hearts Club Band.*

———

It should come as no surprise that Simon and Garfunkel were hot on the heels of the Beatles. Just 10 months after the *Sgt. Pepper* release, they unleashed their own entry in the concept-album sweepstakes. It was called *Bookends.* It had some thematic similarities with *Sgt. Pepper*: "Save the Life of My Child" equals "She's Leaving Home" or "A Day in the Life"; "At the Zoo" equals "Being for the Benefit of Mr. Kite!"; "Old Friends" equals "When I'm Sixty-Four." There were pronounced differences as well. *Pepper* was psychedelic and colorful. *Bookends* was not; it was black and white and gray. The stark black-and-white Richard Avedon photo that adorns the cover perfectly reflects what awaits you inside.

———

Bookends is the album on which Paul's writing and composing talents came to full fruition. All his major themes (youth, alienation, life, love, disillusionment, relationships, old age, and mortality) are represented here in mature, gripping form. It was "the perfect storm" of rock albums—a once-in-a-career convergence of musical, personal, and societal forces that placed Simon and Garfunkel squarely at the center of the cultural zeitgeist of the sixties. *Bookends* came at the height of their musical, personal, and professional partnership and propelled them in that same year to accomplishments greater than had been achieved by any other duo in the history of popular music (including their own idols, the Everly Brothers).

———

To this day, everyone talks about how Bob Dylan "went electric," but with *Bookends*, Simon and Garfunkel went *electrifying*. They elevated the grammar and vocabulary of popular music. They stretched the possibilities of what could be accomplished on a long-playing record. And they reconfigured the emotional, intellectual, and musical limits of rock and roll. In a musical form better known for its primitivism and raw sensuality, these two wrote and sang as if they had brains as well as balls.

And then they *proved* it!

2

THE EARLY YEARS

Our story begins in Queens, New York, in the 1940s. To avoid incurring the wrath of either Mr. Simon or Mr. Garfunkel, I've chosen to place the biographical sketches in this book in alphabetical rather than billing order. This calls to mind the funny, self-deprecating observation Mr. Garfunkel often makes during his solo concerts, usually before performing "Mrs. Robinson," when he says something like "When we were thinking about naming the act, Paul suggested calling the group *Simon and Garfunkel*. I countered by saying that I thought *Garfunkel and Simon* sounded better. Paul demurred, saying, 'To be fair about it, let's do it alphabetically,' and I agreed!"

Though they are not related by blood, the two have exhibited lifelong symptoms of a classic sibling rivalry. Calling it a love–hate relationship is a vast understatement. Nevertheless, at times they even have a sense of humor about this sensitive subject. Once, when we were talking about birthdays, I casually mentioned to Art that although both were born in 1941, Paul is his senior by a matter of weeks. He immediately smiled and, with a gleam in his eye, replied, "He was born 20-something days before me, but he was premature by a month. I was conceived first!" We all laughed. "You'll misunderstand *all* the music if you don't get that!" he continued, to more laughter.

Art is simply one of the most interesting, intelligent, and, yes, eccentric characters ever to have achieved the level of success that he has enjoyed in the recording industry. It isn't easy being Art Garfunkel. Late-night comedians and morning-zoo hosts have had a field day making him the "Ringo-like" fall guy in many Simon and Garfunkel jokes, but make no mistake about it: He was an integral and equal part of one of the most talented and successful duos in music history.

Arthur Ira Garfunkel was born on November 5, 1941, in Forest Hills, Queens, New York. His father, Jacob "Jack" Garfunkel, was a traveling salesman, and his mother, Rose, was a housewife. Art has two siblings, an older brother named Jules and a younger brother named Jerome. He realized at a very early age that he could sing. I must have started singing at about 4 or 5. I remember both of my parents could sing and harmonize to each other, and they would sing 'When the red, red robin comes bob, bob, bobbin' along' or 'Pack up all my care and woe, here I go, singing low—bye-bye blackbird.' And I would hear them do their two-part harmony; and when

I was in kindergarten, I was already singing to myself, and I was aware of going to school, walking on the sidewalks, stepping over the cracks as a first-grader and doing a march tempo to songs; I would be singing to myself, thinking, 'I have a voice!' I would finish the song and then I would do it all over again in a higher key. So I was training. And I was aware that I had this lucky thing that I was trying to make the most of, even as a very young tot."

Having a beautiful voice is one thing; deciding to pursue a career in entertainment is quite another. Garfunkel explains how unlikely his choice really was: "Career and livelihood when you were a kid from my neighborhood in Queens meant to be a lawyer or one of the white-collar professions. So you didn't think 'rock and roll,' and you didn't think 'singing' when you thought of a career. I just did it. And then I did it in the synagogue, and then I sang in talent shows in grade school. By the fourth grade, I was the kid in school who sang, [the one who was] popular with the girls because of being a singer. In the synagogue, you'd wear these white robes and they were satin and shiny—calculated to make you stand out as the neighborhood angel. So I was playing that role by the time I was 8 and 9."

Contrary to popular belief, Paul Simon was *not* born in Queens. He came into the world on October 13, 1941, in

Newark, New Jersey, the first son of Louis and Belle Simon. His father came from a Hungarian Jewish family and, before World War II, had been a violin player on Hungarian radio. After immigrating to the United States, he worked as a bass player to support his growing family. Shortly after Paul was born, the family moved across the Hudson River to settle in the Forest Hills neighborhood of Queens. But then, at the age of 50, Louis decided to make a career change. He went back to school and ultimately earned a doctoral degree in linguistics with a specialty in remedial reading. In 2006, Paul told the *Lebrecht Weekly*:

> My father said to me, I wish I had done this earlier, I wish I hadn't spent so much of my life as a musician. But I liked him as a musician, and I liked his musician friends. It's part of the reason I was able to go into faraway cultures and collaborate with people—not as a foreigner but as a musician among musicians.

Simon's early interest in music and his later explorations of other cultures were sparked by a familiar and cherished household appliance: "I think this comes from the feeling that my generation and all generations that have come after [it have]: We don't have any roots. Our roots are the radio. We're not actually attached to musical cultures. If you just go back one generation before us—

the Everlys, for example—they're from Kentucky. Their father was a country singer. They learned their music from a tradition. Even Elvis Presley, he heard that music. But our generation, we heard it on the radio, and as a kid growing up in Queens, growing up in Forest Hills, I would just flick the dial all the time, listening to different music on the radio. Of course, my favorite was rock and roll—Alan Freed—but I also listened to gospel music that was coming from churches in Brooklyn or Harlem. There was Latin music to be heard. There was even a country station out in New Jersey. So I heard a lot of different music when I was a kid. And I think that concept stayed with me—that anything I heard on the radio was pop music. 'El Condor Pasa' [from *Bridge over Troubled Water*]—that was the first time I really left our culture to investigate music. It happened to be in Peru in this case, but my thinking was, if I like to listen to it, then why should I have a distinction between one kind of music and another?"

Not surprisingly, Art Garfunkel tells a similar story. Art and Paul grew up in the period of our musical history just prior to rock and roll. "The Patti Page days," Art calls them. One day you were asking how much is that doggie in the window, and the next day you were rocking around the clock. Art recalled the bolt out of the blue that was rock and roll in his life:

"Well, one thinks of Alan Freed, the disc jockey, as the godfather, because it was his tremendously dynamic radio style that turned us junior high schoolers on. And what he played, that music seemed decidedly different, very subversive and wonderfully rebellious; and we all, at least those of us who were hip, we jumped onto that track and listened nightly. The big bolt was probably the record itself, and the mood and the flavor of a record such as [the Penguins'] 'Earth Angel.' I think the first time I heard 'Earth Angel' and I just heard that studio sound, I got images of midnight blue colors, and I thought, 'I want to make one of those. I can sing too. Where do you get your hands on the echo?' So that probably was the bolt. Then there was 'Sincerely' by the Moonglows, there was '(I Love You) for Sentimental Reasons' by the Rivileers; but for me, most of all, it was 'Earth Angel' by the Penguins."

And what was the bolt out of the blue for Paul Simon?

"I remember exactly how it happened," he said. "I'm a Yankees fan, so when I was a kid, I would score the Yankees games. I would wait for the games to be broadcast on the radio. I'd be out on the back porch of my house in Queens, and I'd have my scorecard all ready and I'd be writing in the lineup and getting ready to score the game. I was a big Yankees fan, so right before the Yankees came on, there was a show called the *Make Believe Ballroom*. And one day, the disc jockey said, 'Now here's a record that they say is becoming a hit, but it is so bad that if this record is a hit, I will eat it!' The record was 'Gee' by the Crows. 'Oh, Gee.' He puts the record on and I'm filling in [the scorecard]—Mantle, center field; Maris, left field—and 'Gee' by the Crows is playing and I think to myself, 'Hey, I like this. This is pretty good music.' So that was the first rock-and-roll record that I ever heard. It was early rhythm and blues. So that's where I came from. I got into rock and roll. I got hooked. I was into doo-wop. In fact, Artie and I sang in street-corner groups. I began to write rock-and-roll songs, then heard Elvis Presley. Loved that! Then the Everly Brothers, then all of rock and roll."

It makes perfect sense that Paul would single out the Everly Brothers, for a very obvious reason: "Well, the Everly Brothers, I think, are *the* great duo of rock and roll," he said. "Certainly there never would have been a Simon and Garfunkel had there not been an Everly Brothers. That blend of voices was just ... well, I think they are the great rock-and-roll duo. Art and I used to practice singing, and we'd practice singing Everly Brothers songs. Even when we made our first little record, 'Hey, Schoolgirl,' when we were called Tom and Jerry when we were 15 years old, it was very much an imitation of the Everly Brothers. In fact, we put a couple of Everly Brothers songs on our albums—'Bye Bye Love' is on the *Bridge over Troubled Water* album, and we sang 'Wake Up Little Susie' on *Concert in Central Park*. So we learned how to sing together using the Everlys as our guide. I guess there must be something also that I love about those intervals that they sang in—you know, those open fifths and those fourths. There's something about that that I just naturally respond to."

Because they lived just a few blocks away from each other, attended the same schools, and shared an enormous interest in this new music, it was inevitable that Art Garfunkel and Paul Simon would cross paths. Artie told how it happened: "Well, I met him in the sixth grade. I was a singer in the talent shows by the fourth grade. He says he saw me sing and began to realize, 'That's the route to popularity with the girls. You become a singer.' And then by the sixth grade, he was somewhat laying for me in school. So when I first met him and first became aware of this very funny, talented, turned-on kid in my neighborhood, he said, 'You're just meeting me, but I have known about you for a couple of years. I was hoping that you would run into me and that you would think I was neat, so I was pitching for your friendship by the time you met me.'"

The first time they appeared on stage together was in a sixth-grade production of Lewis Carroll's *Alice's Adventures in Wonderland*. Paul was the White Rabbit; Art was the Cheshire Cat! The friendship was now growing into a musical partnership, as well.

Paul and Artie had a short-lived taste of success in the heady days of the early rock-and-roll revolution. The two adopted the pseudonyms of Tom and Jerry. Ironically, in this configuration, Art had top billing as Tom Graph, a name chosen as a nod to his habit of listening to *Your Hit Parade* on the radio on Saturday mornings and keeping

THE EARLY YEARS

detailed charts on graph paper from week to week of the standings of all the hit recordings he heard there; Paul was Jerry Landis, after the surname of a girl he was dating at the time.

Another irony, given that Paul became a solo writer of all Simon and Garfunkel material, is that in the early days they wrote songs *together*! They already knew about the magical blending of their voices. They already had magnetic wire and tape recordings of their versions of Everly Brothers songs. The only ingredient missing from the formula for success in the music business was original material, which they meticulously worked on together.

The early fruit of this collaboration came in 1957. Taking a little bit from Gene Vincent's "Be-Bop-A-Lula" and a little bit from the harmonies of the Everlys, the duo came up with an innocuous little teen trifle called "Hey, Schoolgirl," containing the catchy nonsense opening phrase "Woo-bop-a-loo-chi-ba, you're mine / Woo-bop-a-loo-chi-ba, you're mine." (Clearly, Paul had not yet tapped his considerable talents as the premier American songwriter of his generation!)

The song reached the middle of the national sales charts in the fall of 1957 and went slightly higher on charts for the New York metropolitan area. However, it was eclipsed by monster hit recordings from some of the true first-generation rock-and-roll pioneers and heroes of the day: "That'll Be the Day" by Buddy Holly and the Crickets, "Whole Lot of Shakin' Going On" by Jerry Lee Lewis, the two-sided hit "(Let Me Be Your) Teddy Bear" backed with "Loving You" by Elvis Presley, the two-sided hit "Searchin'" backed with "Young Blood" by the Coasters, and, perhaps most deliciously of all for Art and Paul, "Bye Bye Love" by the Everly Brothers.

You can see from that powerhouse list of hits that the ambitious teens from Queens were in pretty fast company. Unfortunately, it did not last. Their attempts to duplicate the momentum they'd generated with "Hey, Schoolgirl" failed miserably. (Some of the follow-ups in the next year were "Our Song," "Two Teenagers," "Don't Say Goodbye," and "That's My Story.") Tom and Jerry faded quickly from view and were resurrected 7 or 8 years later only as a novelty addendum to the enormous sixties success of Simon and Garfunkel. Artie pinpointed the highlight of the Tom and Jerry experience for him as a Thanksgiving Day 1957 appearance on Dick Clark's *American Bandstand*, broadcast nationally from Phila-delphia on the ABC television network.

The duo took the train down from New York. Dressed in matching red jackets, they lip-synched "Hey, School-girl" for the *American Bandstand* in-studio regulars and the nation. An even bigger thrill for them was the presence of the other guest on that day's program, the Memphis maniac by way of Ferriday, Louisiana, Jerry Lee Lewis, who performed his follow-up to "Whole Lot of Shakin' Going On," the even more lascivious "Great Balls of Fire." Paul has said that they were too nervous to even try to meet him. Unfortunately, kinescopes of the appearance were lost. Paul and Art tried to locate them for the 1969 network television special that they did with the not-yet-so-famous Charles Grodin, but to no avail. Paul has remarked that a recording of almost every other telecast of *American Bandstand* from that era exists in some form, but not the one with Tom and Jerry and Jerry Lee Lewis.

"Hey, Schoolgirl" sold more than 100,000 copies, and Art and Paul split about $4,000 in royalties. Paul used his share to buy a red Chevrolet Impala convertible. It was at least 7 years before the two saw another record company royalty check for work they had done together.

When it became clear that Tom and Jerry had no future, Art and Paul decided that they should redirect their energies and, perhaps, have something to fall back on if their dreams of music-business glory did not work out. Being the practical, intelligent young men that they were, both decided to continue their education and dabble with music on the side. Paul enrolled at Queens College in New York City as an English major but remained active in music, most notably writing songs and making demos with a classmate named Carole Klein. (You may know her better by her stage name, Carole King.) Meanwhile, Artie's fall-back plan was to become an architecture and mathematics student at Columbia University, but he too kept a finger in the music business, releasing two solo singles under the name Artie Garr. They were the teen ballads "Private World" backed with "Forgive Me," and "Beat Love" backed with "Dream Alone" on Octavia and Warwick Records. Neither made a dent on the pop charts.

During this period, tensions between Art and Paul were exacerbated by an incident that took place just after Tom and Jerry broke up. Apparently, Paul did a solo project, which Artie regarded as a betrayal. He has referred to it obliquely with such comments as "Our whole friendship went into suspension over something that happened in those early days. So for about 5 years, we didn't hang out; we weren't each other's friends."

Paul was much more brutal about it in a 1984 interview published in *Playboy* magazine:

> During this time . . . I made a solo record. And it made Artie very unhappy. He looked upon it as something of a betrayal. That sense of betrayal has remained with him. That solo record I made at the age of 15 permanently colored our relationship. We were talking about it recently and I said, "Artie, for Christ's sake, I was 15 years old! How can you carry that betrayal for 25 years? Even if I was wrong, I was just a 15-year-old kid who wanted to be Elvis Presley for one moment instead of being the Everly Brothers with you. Even if you were hurt, let's drop it." But he won't.

And that was the start of a pattern of behavior that repeated itself many times over the next 50 years.

———

THE EARLY YEARS

Let it suffice to say for now that after Tom and Jerry evaporated, Art and Paul spent the next few years trying to find another little hole in the fence around the record business. They wanted another opportunity to get back on the charts, a second chance at the brass ring that in the sixties and seventies came to be called the Big Rock Candy Mountain—a place where international stardom was a given and all your most cherished music-industry wishes came true. That second chance came from a very unlikely source in a very unlikely way—on the coattails of the great American folk boom of the late fifties and early sixties.

3
FOLK

The music business has always been responsive to trends and fads. Any huge, unexpected, original success is immediately followed by a thousand imitators anxious to mine the same vein. The first major post-rock-and-roll trend sprang up in the waning years of the 1950s. The late singer–songwriter–interpreter Dave Van Ronk humorously referred to it as the Great American Folk Scare! It was the revival of a witty, barbed, and intelligent form of music that dealt with *real* people, *real* issues, and *real* cultural traditions. So naturally, Paul Simon and Art Garfunkel were attracted to it.

Folk is the music of the people. And, contrary to popular belief, it is not a curio residing in museum archives. Folk music is *always* with us—just to greater or lesser degrees of visibility. Folk music lives wherever and whenever men and women set rhyming lines to music to express their feelings about life, love, and the human condition. And it has been this way for centuries. British ballads,

Scottish reels, tribal chants, plainsongs, and religious hymns and psalms are all basically folk songs. Immigrants from every corner of the globe brought their culture and native music with them to the New World. Once here, these sounds intermingled, altered, grew, and diversified. Work songs, protest songs, paeons of joy, songs of mourning, prison songs, hollers, love ballads, labor songs, cowboy songs—*all* are folk music, and all can be found, sometimes in traditional form and sometimes in updated fashion, throughout Simon and Garfunkel's esteemed catalog.

The ascension of folk as America's music can be traced to a number of 20th-century pioneers, but perhaps no one had as much influence on it as Woodrow Wilson "Woody" Guthrie, born on July 14, 1912, in Okemah, Oklahoma. Woody is the poster child for American folksingers—a troubadour who rode the rails, took on the Establishment in song, and scrawled "This machine kills Fascists" on the body of his guitar and banjo (a slogan adopted by subsequent performers and musicians from the 1950s onward).

The rise of folk took a great leap forward in 1940 with the formation of the Almanac Singers, which was originally a trio featuring Lee Hays, Millard Lampell, and Pete Seeger. They expanded to a quartet a year later when they added Guthrie. They did an album of labor songs called *Talking Union* in 1941 and an album supporting the World War II effort called *Dear Mr. President* in early 1942, then disbanded in the summer of that year. From the ashes of the Almanac Singers, Woody formed another short-lived group called the Headline Singers (guess what they sang about) with Huddie "Leadbelly" Ledbetter, Sonny Terry, and Brownie McGhee. Lampell then became a writer, and Seeger and Hays joined forces with Ronnie Gilbert and Fred Hellerman to form the phenomenally successful folk quartet the Weavers in 1948.

Without a doubt, the Weavers sparked the great urban folk revival of the 1950s. Their repertoire included faithful renderings of traditional folk standards, rousing originals by Seeger and Hays such as "The Hammer Song (If I Had a Hammer)," and even some slickly produced recordings that became huge bestsellers on the national charts, including "Tzena, Tzena, Tzena," Woody's "So Long, It's Been Good to Know You," and the old Kentucky mountain song "On Top of Old Smokey." A good deal of credit for the quartet's commercial success must go to their producer, Gordon Jenkins, who had a great, lengthy post-Weavers career arranging, conducting, and producing for the likes of Nat "King" Cole, Judy Garland, and Frank Sinatra.

Unfortunately, the Weavers were not able to sustain that level of success because of their head-on collision with one of the darkest periods of American history. The communist-baiting pamphlet *Red Channels* labeled the group provocateurs and subversives, and in the stifling, witch-hunting atmosphere promoted by Senator Joseph McCarthy of Wisconsin, the Weavers were blacklisted and driven off the national stage that had so warmly welcomed them. As a result of these pressures, the group disbanded in 1953. It was a sorry chapter in American social, political, and musical history, but it has in no way threatened the group's rightful place in the vanguard of the great mid-20th-century American folk revival.

One of the *most* visible periods of the folk explosion started in the late 1950s. It dovetailed with the emergence of a clean-cut threesome called the Kingston Trio, formed in San Francisco in 1957. Dave Guard, Nick Reynolds, and Bob Shane put together a very slick package of traditional folk songs mixed with fan-friendly originals that took the charts and the country by storm. Folk purists blanched, but the economic viability of polished, commercial folk music was undeniable. In November 1958, the trio's version of a traditional Appalachian murder ballad called "Tom Dooley" topped the pop charts in the United States and then all around the world.

Just when LPs were becoming the major sales vehicles for the burgeoning record industry, the Kingston Trio began a run on the album charts that saw five of their first six albums make it to number one on the U.S. charts. They were on the cover of *Life* magazine and featured in *Time*.

The hit-making formula the trio devised was not lost on a generation of talented, struggling, somewhat opportunistic musicians. The Kingston Trio's success paved the way for a succession of coed folk acts in various permutations. There were soloists, duos, trios, quartets, and, in some cases, many-member ensembles such as the New Christy Minstrels and the Au Go Go Singers (which at one time included future Buffalo Springfield members Richie Furay and Stephen Stills). Folk Madonnas in peasant blouses were everywhere. Protest singers were pointing fingers in every direction. Troubadours dressed in work shirts and carrying guitars were falling all over one another. Distinctive folk scenes sprang up and thrived in Boston, Chicago, Los Angeles, and San Francisco, but the mecca for this type of music was smack in the heart of New York City's Greenwich Village. The clubs, the coffeehouses, the parks, and even the street corners were filled with aspiring folkies.

The talent pool was pretty large, and the trend did not go unnoticed by the movers and shakers in management, concert promotion, and the recording industry's executive suites. The major companies already had a toehold in the folk boom, and they were followed by newer independent labels, such as Elektra and Vanguard, that had been formed to nurture and serve it. Music impresario Albert Grossman (immortalized in the Paul Simon send-up "A Simple Desultory Philippic") even created, Svengali-like, a folk supergroup. He put a Cornell University singer–songwriter together with an up-and-coming stand-up comedian and musician from Baltimore and a lissome blonde with a great voice from New York City. Peter Yarrow, Noel "Paul" Stookey, and Mary Travers became an instant sensation with the release of their debut album in 1962. Their success soared to even greater heights when Grossman gave them some songs for their second album that were written by a client of his who called himself Bob Dylan. In fact, one could say that Peter, Paul and Mary's hit version of "Blowin' in the Wind," which reached number two on the pop charts in 1963, blew the doors open for the scruffy balladeer from Hibbing, Minnesota. Just about everyone who was interested in music began to take notice.

So, oddly enough, it wasn't rock and roll that brought Simon and Garfunkel back together; it was folk music. This resilient form of musical expression was once again a very visible tree in the music-industry forest, and two young men in Queens who had gone their separate ways were independently drawn to it.

Paul's story: "By the time you got to the end of the fifties and the early sixties, the music wasn't so great, and I started to drift away from listening to rock and roll. But what was happening in New York was that there was a very, very interesting folk scene happening down in Greenwich Village around Bleecker and MacDougal Streets. I used to go down to hootenannies at Gerde's Folk City. And so I started to listen to these old Weavers and Woody Guthrie records and Pete Seeger, then Joan Baez. I said, 'Enough of this teen rock and roll. It's just awful. I'm into folk.' So I hung around the folk scene, but I couldn't find anyplace to play, because you had to come from North Dakota or Tennessee, and Queens was just not a hip place to come from if you wanted to be a folksinger."

Art's story: "From my point of view, it started with the Kingston Trio [and] 'Tom Dooley.' It moved on to groups like the Brothers Four and 'Greenfields,' the Limelighters, and then came Joan Baez—a terrific soprano with these beautiful English child ballads. That's what began to hook me. When I began to hear these English ballads, I started getting interested in that music. And then came Bob Dylan, who had this wonderful image as well as this talent to write these kinds of things. And from Dylan came Paul's writing style in that fashion, and then came the two of us doing those songs."

A lot of Dylan's early work was categorized as protest music, but Artie didn't see it that way. "I didn't hear protest songs," he said. "I heard lyrics with a point, that's what I heard. The lyrics had woken up. Prior to that, I had never heard lyrics that had any of the energy and the exclamation point that these began to have. That, to me, was the new thing. Songs, which were always words and music, now had words in a very dynamic sense, and music. They had never used that power of what words could do before."

Disappointed with the lukewarm reception he was getting in his hometown, Paul Simon took a dramatic step: "Shortly after Kennedy was assassinated in '63, I left the country and traveled around through Europe. I took my guitar with me, and I used to sing on the streets, make money singing on the streets, like in Paris or Amsterdam. You could go out and play, get enough money to buy break-fast or dinner, or get enough money to find a place to stay that night. It was sort of a kid community of people hitch-hiking through Europe and playing. And the music that I was playing was the folk music that I heard on records. I met an English kid named David McCauslind, and he said, 'Well, if you come over to England, you could come and stay with my family.' So I went there and I began to sing at little English folk clubs. These were actually rooms above a pub. Gradually, I got more bookings, because in England, the reverse was true of what I had experienced in New York. To be an American in England in 1963 was to be exotic, whereas to be from Forest Hills in New York in 1963 was to be . . . ragweed. So I said, 'Hey, I'm having a better time in England. I'm going to stay here.' And I did. I'd sort of go back and forth between there and here."

Paul wrote one of his most commercially successful songs while he was in Europe. It was called "Red Rubber Ball." A live version by Simon and Garfunkel ultimately appeared on their *Old Friends* box set, but the hit single was recorded by a group called the Cyrkle in 1966, and it climbed to the number-two position on the American charts. The seeds for this circuitous route to success had been planted at least 2 years earlier. "I wrote that song when I was living in England," Paul said, "and I just wrote it for the money. This was before Simon and Garfunkel, and I needed rent money. I knew I could get a 100-pound advance if I wrote this song for a group called the Seekers. They were an Australian group that was very popular in England at the time. So I cowrote it with one of the Seekers [Bruce Woodley], which was a way that I could be assured of having the Seekers record the song. Then I could get an advance of 100 pounds, which was a pretty good amount of money in those days, and that was it. I never thought about it again, and they did sing it. Then the Cyrkle covered the Seekers, and that became a big hit record. I think it's the only song I ever wrote like a commercial—you know, 'Pay me and I'll write a song.' Of course, I never anticipated that it would be that big of a hit. So it becomes a rock-and-roll trivia question: 'Who wrote "Red Rubber Ball"?'"

Meanwhile, Paul Simon and Art Garfunkel's partnership, which had remained in a state of suspended animation for about 5 years, showed signs of life again in 1963, when they reconnected over their mutual interest in this new music scene that was swirling around them. Art told Paul Zollo in 1990:

> When we next got back together again, we were really on different footing. You know, those are very critical years in your development. So we were more advanced, collegiate types then, and now the world knew of this thing called Bob Dylan and Joan Baez and all that folky stuff.

Paul says simply, "Then came Bob Dylan, and it starts to get really interesting. So I began to write songs in that style." "That style" could certainly be called Dylanesque. Art's responses to hearing songs by Paul such as "He Was My Brother" ("the innocent voice of an uncomfortable youth"), "Sparrow" ("The song is asking, 'Who will love?' Poetic personification is used for the answers."), and "Bleecker Street" ("the first appearance of a theme that is to occupy great attention in later work—'lack of communication'") led him to believe that he and Paul could have another chance for success in the record business. He told Paul Zollo:

> And then we started harmonizing them and we were giddy with joy over how appealing it was to our own ears. Before the world gets to know something that's neat, *you* get to know it. And you're your own spectator of what's coming out of you. And it's really kind of delirious and happy. It made you want to giggle while you were singing, and it was so much fun doing these things.

In the midst of this creative renaissance, the rivalry and bad feelings were put aside and the reconstituted duo, this time proudly calling themselves by their own last names, began a full-court press to get back in the business and on the charts. It didn't happen overnight, but it was a start.

———

On one of Paul's trips back home from England, fate and synchronicity intervened in a big way. "I took a job [in New York] very briefly working for a music publisher," Paul said. "I didn't like the job. It was an unsatisfying thing to do. My job was to go around with songs that this publishing house published and try to get other people to record them. In the course of this, I had to go up to Columbia Records to try and sell these songs. I met Tom Wilson, who was a producer at Columbia Records. He was producing Bob Dylan and another group called the Pilgrims. I showed him some of [the publisher's songs] and he said, 'I'd like to get these songs to the Pilgrims to record.' I said to Tom, 'Well, I have a friend. We sing together and I'd like to do an audition for Columbia.' He said, 'All right.' So we came in, Art Garfunkel and I, and we sang four or five songs. Columbia Records signed us, much to our shock, and that's when we made this first record, *Wednesday Morning, 3 A.M.*"

One very important footnote to this story is that the engineer for Art and Paul's demo session was a Columbia staffer, Roy Halee, who would play a key role in Simon's and Garfunkel's futures, both collectively and individually. But credit for the "big break" has to go to the late, great producer and visionary Tom Wilson.

Thomas Blanchard Wilson Jr. was born on March 25, 1931, and grew up in Waco, Texas. While attending Harvard University, he worked for its radio station, WHRB, which he once credited for all his success in the music industry. After graduating, he set his sights on a career in the record business and worked at Savoy, United Artists, and Audio Fidelity before landing a staff producer job at Columbia in 1963.

At the time, he was about the only black record producer working for a mainstream American popular-music record company, but his real claim to fame is the artists he discovered, worked with, nurtured, and took from obscurity to legendary status in the sixties and seventies. The list includes Bob Dylan, the Blues Project, Frank Zappa and the Mothers of Invention, and the Velvet Underground. By any measure, that's an astonishing résumé, but adding to it the success of Simon and Garfunkel makes it almost unbelievable.

The sessions for the album took place in the spring of 1964. The finished product, called *Wednesday Morning, 3 A.M.* after the 12th and last song on the LP, was as folkie as they come. Much like Bob Dylan's debut in 1962, the album contained traditional folk songs ("Peggy-O," "Go Tell It on the Mountain"), covers of songs by contemporaries writing in that style (Ed McCurdy's "Last Night I Had the Strangest Dream" and Bob Dylan's "The Times

They Are a-Changin'"), and five Paul Simon originals, including an acoustic and very folkie version of a song called "The Sound of Silence." After the vocals were done, Paul went off to Europe to travel and perform as a solo act, while Art stayed behind to continue his studies at Columbia University and oversee the finishing touches on the album.

Tom Wilson asked Artie to write the liner notes for the album. At first he was reluctant, because he felt that Paul should explain his own songs. But then he warmed up to the idea and embraced the task with typical Garfunkelian enthusiasm. In a letter to Paul in England, he wrote:

> I know how you feel about this, but I (your greatest advocate) want as many as possible to understand as much as possible. Please understand that mine is the difficult position more than slightly analogous to the man who received Franz Kafka's dying request to burn all his manuscripts, but who nonetheless felt obliged to rush off to the publisher at his first chance. The point is that you understanding the songs, me believing in their worth, and Columbia recording them is really not sufficient. So I decided last night to write the following as a "listener's guide to the songs."

He reserved his greatest praise for the closing track on side one:

"The Sound of Silence" is a major work. We were looking for a song on a larger scale, but this was more than either of us expected. Paul had the theme and the melody set in November, but 3 months of frustrating attempts were necessary before the song "burst forth." On February 19, 1964, the song practically wrote itself.

When he was asked many years later to assess that first album, Art said, "We were trying to be this clean-cut folkie group. It's a little false to who we were in those times. Some of the songs we were doing there were [done] as if we were trying to get on the label, or letting the manager we were working with at the time influence us toward certain tunes. I would probably shy away from aspects of it if I were to hear it now. 'Go Tell It on the Mountain' is typical of the songs that I'm talking about. I wouldn't do it again if it weren't for the fact that others said it should be done. I think 'The Sun Is Burning' is an interesting nuclear-war song typical of those times."

The fate of *Wednesday Morning, 3 A.M.* and Simon and Garfunkel's pure folkie days met with a pretty abrupt judgment in late 1964. Paul summed it up succinctly when he said, "The record came out. It wasn't a hit. I moved back to England to work in the clubs."

4

FOLK ROCK

"The Sound of Silence" may have written itself on February 19, 1964, as Artie suggests, but the sounds in America exactly 10 days earlier had been anything but silence. Those were the sounds of the Beatles on the *Ed Sullivan Show* on Sunday evening, February 9, 1964. One of the most-watched programs in the history of American broadcast television, that single appearance opened the floodgates for a new kind of music that would soon engulf the colonies. But the so-called British Invasion was not really about original music. It was more about adopting and co-opting American rock and roll, reinventing it, and throwing it back to us across the pond in new and unique and original forms.

Take any group that made its mark that year—the Beatles, the Rolling Stones, the Kinks, the Yardbirds, the Dave Clark Five, etc.—and you'll find this to be true. Other than the Beatles, only three British acts had number-one singles in 1964: Peter and Gordon with

Lennon and McCartney's "World Without Love," Manfred Mann with American songwriters Jeff Barry and Ellie Greenwich's "Do Wah Diddy," and Eric Burdon and the Animals with a cover version of the traditional "House of the Rising Sun" (for which the arrangement was lifted from Bob Dylan's debut album; Dylan, in turn, had lifted it from one of his early mentors, Dave Van Ronk).

The Animals electrified and propelled to number one on the American charts this early example of what came to be known the next year as folk rock. That audacious version of "House of the Rising Sun" did not escape the interest of *Saturday Morning, 3 A.M.* producer Tom Wilson. In fact, he experimented with electrifying Dylan's version, but he abandoned the attempt and never released the result. But the crafty Mr. Wilson obviously had this notion in mind early on and did not hesitate to try it again. (He would get his chance a year later.)

Folk continued to do well on the American charts, even after the onslaught of the British Invasion began. Top-10 folk recordings in 1964 included "Don't Let the Rain Come Down" by the Serendipity Singers, "We'll Sing in the Sunshine" by Gale Garnett, and even "Summer Song" by the British duo Chad and Jeremy, but *Wednesday Morning, 3 A.M.* sank without a trace. Discouraged by the failure but accustomed to the vagaries of the record business, Simon and Garfunkel shrugged their shoulders and accepted their fate. Paul went back to

England, Art went back to school, and the story could have ended right there—but it didn't.

———

The dawning of 1965 brought a new wrinkle, a new sound to the table—folk rock.

Folk rock is the very simple and accurate term used to describe the marriage of traditional folk music and American rock and roll, which took place on a very large scale in the mid-sixties. What rock liked about folk was its lyrical depth, musical textures, and emotional intensity. What folk liked about rock was its electricity (literally and figuratively), sense of excitement and fun, and direct access to a ready and waiting mass audience. In fact, folk rock provided a vehicle for making powerful statements and sending meaningful messages to an audience larger than had been available for each form separately.

What combined them? A pretty potent one-two punch is what did it: the reinvention of Bob Dylan as a rock-and-roll star and the emergence of a five-man group called the Byrds, whose members were described in their early public relations campaign as America's answer to the Beatles. There were other folk-rock hit makers in 1965—the Turtles, Sonny and Cher, and the Lovin' Spoonful among them—but it was Dylan's influence on the Byrds and vice versa that made the entire movement percolate.

Dylan was the prime mover of this new hybrid. He released two albums in 1965 (both produced by Tom

Wilson), *Bringing It All Back Home* in March and *Highway 61 Revisited* in August. The former contained Dylan's first recorded experimentation with the form, "Subterranean Homesick Blues," and the latter was full-tilt electrified folk rock. To do justice to the size of the accomplishment these records represented, I repeat: In the course of *just 5* months in 1965, Bob Dylan released *two* of the most successful, innovative, influential, layered, textured, adventurous long-playing albums in the history of rock and roll or any other recorded music. Whew!

The earlier of the two was a transitional album on which Dylan had one foot in the acoustic waters he had navigated so successfully on his first four albums. (Did he entitle it *Bringing It All Back Home* to acknowledge his return to the beloved rock and roll he had embraced as a teenager?) The later album was his first all-out, full-tilt electrified rock-and-roll album, and it was led off and spearheaded by the song that has been recently described as the single most important recording of the 20th century—"Like a Rolling Stone." It was followed by pile drivers in their own right such as "Ballad of a Thin Man," the title song, and "Just Like Tom Thumb's Blues." All 6 minutes of "Like a Rolling Stone" made it to the number-two spot on the American pop charts in the late summer of '65, and performers everywhere began searching through the already large catalog of songs Dylan had written to find the ones they could turn into rock-and-roll hits. But that, too, had already happened.

Folk rock hurtled into the public consciousness in 1965 with the release of a single by a group originally called the Jet Set, then the Beefeaters, and, finally, the Byrds. Gene Clark, Michael Clarke, David Crosby, Chris Hillman, and Jim McGuinn (who later changed his first name to Roger) each brought something unique to the group. Their combined influences included bluegrass, blues, country, folk, jazz, and rock and roll. The musical credentials were solid, but they also had three traits that were very appealing to young record buyers, particularly the females among them, in the 1960s: great looks, great locks, and great licks! After a couple of false starts with other labels (including the folk haven Elektra), the Byrds were signed to Columbia and assigned a staff producer by the name of Terry Melcher (son of the very popular film star Doris Day).

McGuinn knew his way around folk music, but he also understood the powerful appeal of the new breed of British rock groups led by the Beatles. After seeing George Harrison play a Rickenbacker 12-string electric guitar in *A Hard Day's Night* on a summer evening in 1964, McGuinn added one to his formidable arsenal of instruments. The last piece needed to complete the puzzle was a strong song to put out as a single. As luck would have it, the group's manager, Jim Dickson, who was friendly with several members of Bob Dylan's entourage, had received an early demo of a Dylan song slated for *Bringing It All Back Home* called "Mr. Tambourine Man." It was a long, imagistic acoustic song that probably had no chance of being a hit single with Dylan's arrangement, which included slightly off-key harmonies by Ramblin' Jack Elliott.

After some initial reluctance, McGuinn came up with a couple of ideas that totally transformed the song. He dropped a couple of verses to make it more manageable and bring it down to "single size" (2:10, in this case) and added a stunning instrumental opening played on his 12-string electric that to this day remains one of the most unique announcements of an important group's arrival ever captured on record. "Mr. Tambourine Man" quickly ascended to number one on the American charts in June 1965, and folk rock achieved instant "new phenomenon" status. Dylan "plugged in" at the Newport Folk Festival in July, and "Like a Rolling Stone" rocketed into the top 10 by the end of the summer. The mad scramble for other folk-rock hits was on.

Tom Wilson watched all of this happening at Columbia Records and remembered that one of the songs he had produced on that album by Simon and Garfunkel in 1964 had generated a lot of interest in select markets around the country, most notably Boston and Florida. Without notifying Paul or Art, he went back into the original tracks for the album and (much as he had with Dylan's "House of the Rising Sun" the year before) added 12-string guitar, drum, and electric bass tracks to "The Sound of Silence" and released the new version as a single. This isn't as far-fetched as it seems. Rock and Roll Hall of Famer Dion DiMucci told me that, at Wilson's behest, he and some fine New York studio musicians had done the same thing to an early acoustic solo demo of Dylan's "Maggie's Farm." He swears that the subsequently released album version was a direct lift from the track that he and an electrified rhythm section had recorded that day. Author Fred Bronson claims in the *Billboard Book of Number One Hits* that after producing the legendary mid-June session for Dylan's "Like a Rolling Stone," Wilson asked some of the musicians to stay behind to work on another song. It was, of course, "The Sound of Silence." When Artie first heard the electrified mix, he said, "[They] played it for me in September of 1965 when I had just come back from England ready to return to school. Paul stayed on in England. [They took] 'The Sound of Silence' off the *Wednesday Morning* folk album, added the electric 12-string guitar, the drums, and the bass, and put it in the folk-rock sound that the Byrds were using with 'Turn! Turn! Turn!' and that high treble, twangy, but good rock-and-roll rhythm style of that time. I said, 'It's interesting. I suppose it might do something. It might sell,' but I was conditioned at that point to never having any hits, so I didn't really expect anything."

By the fall of 1965, the song was climbing the U.S. charts and Art Garfunkel had the happy task of tracking down Paul Simon in Europe and urging him to come home to America because the duo finally had their long-coveted, bona fide top-40 hit! Shortly after performing his "fairy godfather" role in resurrecting "The Sound of Silence," Tom Wilson left Columbia for a lucrative position at MGM/Verve Records, where he continued his amazing winning streak with talents such as Frank Zappa and the Mothers of Invention, the Blues Project, and the Velvet Underground. Another Columbia staffer, Bob Johnston, took over as producer for Art and Paul.

There had been "accidental" hits before, like when deejays flipped over a single and made the "B" side a hit rather than the "A" side (Gene Vincent's "Be-Bop-A-Lula" was a B side that became a hit instead of the A side, "Woman Love"), or when a failed single used in a public service announcement made an unexpected, dramatic return to the charts ("Get Together" by the Youngbloods). The story of "The Sound of Silence" is in a class by itself, though, not only because of the improbable means by which it became a hit, but also because it marked the beginning of the dramatic and long-lasting careers of our two urban troubadours, both collectively and individually.

An amazing coda punctuates the ending of our story about the breakthrough of these highly intelligent, multi-talented, very focused and determined future Rock and Roll Hall of Famers. Needless to say, Paul heeded Artie's advice and quickly returned to the States upon hearing about the unlikely success of "The Sound of Silence." Here's the story in his own words from his 1986 visit to my *Mixed Bag* radio program: "Well, I came back from England, and the record was, like, number eight—this overdubbed record that I didn't really have much to do with. I didn't have a place to stay, so I moved back into my parents' house in Queens. And Artie was still living out in Queens, too. One night, Artie and I are sitting out in my car parked on a corner having a smoke. I think we were sitting out on the corner of 70th Road and 141st Street. 'The Sound of Silence' comes on the radio and the disc jockey says, 'Number-one record, Simon and Garfunkel!' And Artie turns to me and he says, 'I'll bet those guys are having a *great* time!'"

For years now, Paul has been telling this story about how he and Art discovered that they had a number-one single. But the lighter side of the "sibling" rivalry between these two is evident when Artie said, with tongue planted firmly in cheek, "I'm sure whatever Paul said is the true story, and I certainly would not even attempt to give another one." After much laughter, he, of course, proceeded to tell a completely different version of finding out about the song becoming number one: "It gives you the feeling, and I remember this feeling very well, that there is no one in America who has a song more popular than our song. That was great fun. It leaped from [number] five to one that week—December something, 1965. We were in L.A. Our manager called us at the hotel we were staying at. We were both in the same room. We must have bunked in the same room in those days. I picked up the phone. He said, 'Well, congratulations. Next week you will go from five to one in *Billboard*.' It was fun. I remember pulling open the curtains and letting the brilliant sun come into this very red room, and then ordering room service. That was good."

———

Paul likes to punctuate his version by stating, "The rest, as they say, is . . . boring!" But the truth is that the rest was anything *but* boring. Without even trying, Simon and Garfunkel were handed a leading role in the sixties rock revolution right alongside all the other heavy hitters (Dylan, the Beatles, McGuinn, et al.). In recent years, some music historians have tried to minimize the importance of folk rock, but for many people, myself included, it was one of the more significant elements in the maturation of this "rebel music." Paul agrees: "Folk rock was a little cul-de-sac, I guess. It really has to be thought of as sixties music. You have to think of the Beatles and you have to think of the Stones. They also were influenced by it. Folk rock was the first time that rock and roll talked about life, talked about white middle-class life, street life. The Beatles were the first group to smoke a cigarette in front of a camera. You have to think to Elvis Presley when everything about his life was hidden. He had to be this pure image. The Beatles and the Stones—these were like

———

bad boys. And folk rock introduced the idea that lyrics could be real and that they could be even enriched language, or even approach poetic language."

In his 1986 visit to my radio program, Paul spoke passionately about how rock and roll had needed to grow up and break loose from the simplistic teenage label that had been pinned on it in the early days. And he was certain that the evolution of folk rock had a lot to do with this so-called "kid's music" starting to be perceived as a more serious, adult form of musical expression: "Rock and roll as I remember it from my earliest days, and from every generation that has followed, has become the basic musical language. It strikes me that it was the perfect vocabulary to begin with. You can always go back and find the heart through rock and roll because we all heard it when we were at that age when we were vulnerable and available. Our heart was wide open to it . . . This is true of every generation that has followed, because rock and roll has always been here, so every generation of adolescents comes along and finds that those changes, that beat, will get to them. But if the music remains only on an adolescent level, then those of us who are now older, have grown older, we lose a means of talking to each other. I have a son . . . he listens to rock and roll. I listen to rock and roll. We actually have a subject that we can talk about, and it is probably our main subject that we find we can talk about.

"The generation that is pre–rock and roll is very different," he continued. "After rock and roll, no matter what the differences are, there's a tremendous similarity . . . So what the sixties did was, it was the first time the music had grown up to be not 14-year-olds', 15-year-olds' music, but music of 25-year-olds, because that was our age. And because it was music for 25-year-olds, it was more intellectually curious, and it meant that there were college people in there, and it meant that . . . Bob Dylan took his name from Dylan Thomas, who was a poet. This is the first time that some major cultural figure said, 'Look, a poet is very important.' That is something that shouldn't really be given up. I feel we happen to be living in particularly vacuous times, spiritually, very threadbare times. And there's very little in the music that will comfort people who are older than adolescents. I think this accounts in part for the enormous popularity of artists like Bruce Springsteen, John Mellencamp, Bob Seger. They're actually talking about a certain kind of life. It happens to be small town and blue collar—that kind of American life. But it is at least trying to be real about it, and is talking about it as if it is important, which it is. There are many aspects of our life that should be addressed in the music, and we shouldn't lose this music as a way of talking about what it is like to be alive today."

Simon and Garfunkel are often included in that select group of artists called the architects of folk rock. But Paul disavows any such notion. "No. I don't really think that's so, because the idea really came out of McGuinn, Dylan . . . We should probably credit David Crosby in here, too. I had been writing songs since I was 13, and at that time I was writing songs in the style of folk rock. I don't really feel that I found my own voice until [later]. We drew from many sources, but we didn't invent any of the sources. We came off the streets of New York, so we knew about doo-wop and rock and roll, and we were able to sing all those big background parts. We knew about harmony from the Everlys. We knew about making records because we had started going around knocking on doors when we were 14 and we made our first record when we were 15. We knew about folk music because I was living in England and [was] part of the English folk scene. And we were able to combine all those elements into something that became very popular. But we didn't invent any of those elements. We were absorbers of it and synthesizers of those elements."

The story of "The Sound of Silence" becoming a hit almost by accident is a strange one even for the record business. Art has a fairly nonchalant take on it: "I think the lesson to learn is that most of the big events in our lives happen in this sort of [way that is] after the fact, someone else put it together quite by accident and picked things that are now passé for you. Then it appealed to others. This kind of after-the-fact, accidental way is really what leads to all kinds of major happenings in people's lives, which is almost to say that you never really get the planned-for results of what you work on. It's just always something else. All you can do, I guess, is just be busy

FOLK ROCK

working per se and then hope that something comes of that at some point in some way back at you later on. This is what happened with ["The Sound of Silence"].

Perhaps the question to ask here is whether "talent will out." Not necessarily. For every performing artist who makes it to the top, countless talented unknowns never get there and—like Harry Chapin's Mr. Tanner—end up singing to themselves after-hours in their cleaning shop in Dayton, Ohio. What factors make the difference? Talent is the given, but then it boils down to dogged determination, terrific timing, and, maybe most important of all, a landslide's worth of luck. The stars and planets have to line up in a precise configuration to give birth to the next celestial superstar. And that is *exactly* what happened for Simon and Garfunkel late in 1965. But that was only the beginning.

"The Sound of Silence" could have been just another one-hit wonder, cashing in on the trendy real estate that folk rock had on the American charts in 1965. There had been others along the way: "You Were on My Mind" by a group called We Five, a folk-rock cover of Sylvia Fricker's folk tune, and "Elusive Butterfly" by Bob Lind. There were also groups that used folk rock as a launching pad, then quickly moved into the more commercial pop-rock category. This list includes the Turtles, who made their mark with a folk-rock cover of Bob Dylan's "It Ain't Me Babe" but enjoyed greater success with frothier pop tunes such as "Happy Together," which was a number-one single for the group in 1967. Also on this list is Sonny and Cher. "I Got You Babe" was certainly one of the defining folk-rock hits of 1965, and the duo continued to mine that vein with Cher's cover of Dylan's "All I Really Want to Do" and Sonny Bono's own personal protest manifesto, "Laugh at Me."

Simon and Garfunkel may have gotten back into the record business in a roundabout, lucky fashion, but once they were handed the opportunity, they made the most of it. Art was as surprised as anyone that their retooled folkie song became such a big hit, but he clearly knew how to handle it. "It's an oddity that it was a year and a half old then. The group as a duo was pretty much nonexistent at that point. So we said, now we are [a duo]. Let's do it. Let's get the follow-up hit!"

With the advantage of hindsight, it's fascinating to observe the revolving door of the pop-music business. Basically, there are three categories of stars: Dashers, Sprinters, and Long-Distance Runners. The Dashers are the one- or two-hit wonders who don't stick around for very long but can resurface once in a while on the oldies circuit (if singing the same song over and over and over again doesn't drive them crazy). The Sprinters usually have a cluster of hits over a very specific period of time, but then the well dries up. If the group decides to stay together in one form or another, they can make a respectable living touring well beyond the shelf life of their hits. The third group is the most interesting of all. The Long-Distance Runner's body of work is so influential and profound that it transcends time and eventually even mortality. The Long-Distance Runners are the movers and shakers of the music industry both as a business and an art. The best of them set the bar for all those who follow in their wake, and they continue to affect the culture long after they decide to stop performing and—again, in some cases—even after their death. Simon and Garfunkel are Long-Distance Runners.

"The Sound of Silence" was the starting line on Simon and Garfunkel's long-distance track. In that era, the two main goals after having a hit single that came out of nowhere were to get another one as fast as you could and to put out an album as quickly as possible to cash in on the success of the hit. *The Sounds of Silence* album was recorded in about 3 weeks and released by Columbia on January 17, 1966.

There is a legend in the record business about the so-called "sophomore jinx." The theory is that an artist has years to write and produce his or her first album, then 2 months to do the second. All too often, the pressures of such an endeavor have resulted in work that is less artistically and commercially successful—ergo, the "sophomore jinx." Simon and Garfunkel had no such problem. First of all, *The Sounds of Silence* album was not really a follow-up to *Wednesday Morning, 3 A.M.* Second, Paul had a backlog of strong material that could quickly be recorded, produced, and released, and those songs could stand shoulder to shoulder with the hit-single title track. It may have been recorded more quickly than they would have liked, but it splendidly accomplished the goals of getting an album on the market and putting another single on the charts. The album was a hit, rising to number 26. "And," as they used to say in top-40 radio, "the hits just kept on coming." The follow-up single to "The Sound of Silence" was a solid success, as well. It was a song that Paul had written at a train station in England called "Homeward Bound," and it too rose to the upper reaches of the American charts in the winter of 1966, finally settling in at number five. They didn't waste any time in those days, and Columbia quickly released "I Am a Rock" as the third single from *The Sounds of Silence* in May. The result? Another smash. It stayed on the charts for 10 weeks and reached number three.

A slight miscalculation was made in choosing the next single, "The Dangling Conversation," which soon appeared on *Parsley, Sage, Rosemary and Thyme*. The song was another uncompromising Paul Simon commentary about a dissolving relationship, awash with poetic imagery and serious intellectual concerns ("Can analysis be worthwhile? Is the theater really dead?"). It was their lowest-charting single, getting no higher than number 25, and it stayed on the charts for only 4 weeks. Art told Paul Zollo:

> Yeah. We thought, "Can we take the audience where we want to go now and do a ballad?" Because ballads are tougher to have hits on. Something slow and really intellectual and literary. Let's see if they'll go for that, because then we can take them anywhere. It turned out that we couldn't. That record was not a hit . . . You start thinking of songs in two categories: singles and album cuts . . . So, certainly for singles, we knew it was best to stay away from the long, intellectual ballad.

Another one of the spoils of having a hit record is the ability to make a lot of money touring (in addition to advances and royalties). And tour they did, playing mostly weekends and mostly at colleges, but with such low overhead (two voices, one acoustic guitar) that it could be very rewarding financially. No flash-in-the-pan, one-hit wonder, Simon and Garfunkel had their fingers on the pulse of the sixties. They were urban, smart, sophisticated, erudite, ambitious, and true believers in beloved rock and roll. They also knew that it had far more potential for artistic expression in that decade than it had had in the previous one. In the midst of all this, ideas for another album began brewing. It would not be a quickie like *The Sounds of Silence* but rather one with lofty and artistic visions and ambitions.

Work on *Parsley, Sage, Rosemary and Thyme* began in 1966 and took about 9 months. On September 7, Paul and Art went into the studio to record a single that did not appear on *Parsley, Sage.* Called "A Hazy Shade of Winter," it climbed to number 13 on the national charts. Although it didn't crack the top 10, this fact was completely overshadowed by the critical acclaim for and commercial success of *Parsley, Sage, Rosemary and Thyme* after its release in October. It surpassed anything the duo had done previously and offered stunning evidence of their many talents, as well as tantalizing hints of untapped potential.

The album begins with one of the most beautiful and satisfying songs the two ever did together. "It opens with 'Scarborough Fair,'" Artie said, "which I think is the most natural, flowing, organic thing we ever did. I just loved the 3 days we spent doing that [track]. I remember so well how it sort of wrote itself as a record." He also felt that it was the moment when they first took the reins of another part of the process: "We became producers. We were not only on mike in the studio but back behind the glass at the dials, mixing along with Roy Halee. We produced it with Roy and called our own shots in terms of instrumentation . . . Really, it's in the album that you can expand and do a lot of creative things . . . So I felt we were entering into the art of album making at that point, which is something above and beyond songwriting and singing."

It had a little bit of everything people had come to expect from Simon and Garfunkel: strikingly beautiful singing and guitar playing ("For Emily, Whenever I May Find Her"); blisteringly satirical lyrics aimed at a multitude of pop-culture targets ("The Big Bright Green Pleasure Machine" and "A Simple Desultory Philippic"); playful optimism ("The 59th Street Bridge Song"); contemplations on self-identity ("Patterns" and "Flowers Never Bend with the Rainfall"); and breathtaking slice-of-life vignettes that stopped listeners in their tracks ("A Poem on the Underground Wall" and "7 o'Clock News/ Silent Night").

Few others have come even close to the intelligence, beauty, variety, creativity, and craftsmanship that *Parsley, Sage, Rosemary and Thyme* captured. Simon and Garfunkel at the end of 1966 were poised to scale even greater heights in both the artistic and commercial aspects of the recording industry.

5

1967

In January 1967, Paul and Art returned once again to the studio for singles duty. It was a song called "At the Zoo," and it stands as another perfect example of Paul Simon's ability to effortlessly throw together whimsical commentary, surreal images, and catchy hooks and rhythms that genuinely delight listeners of all ages. "At the Zoo" peaked at number 16 on the singles charts, making it two in a row that didn't crack the top 10, but it hardly mattered because Simon and Garfunkel had moved way beyond the folk-rock stereotype. With the release of *Parsley, Sage, Rosemary and Thyme*, they took their place alongside the most talented rock auteurs of the period.

Their timing was perfect. The significance of the Rock Revolution could no longer be ignored. Scorned and dismissed just a decade earlier, rock and roll was now applauded, rewarded, and accorded intensely serious analysis and great critical praise. In a CBS network news special called *Inside Pop: The Rock Revolution* that aired on April 25, 1967, no less an eminence than Leonard Bernstein gave the new rock his unconditional blessing. The Museum of Television and Radio describes the show in this brief synopsis: "An enthusiastic Leonard Bernstein hosts this special program, intended to shed light on the exploding cultural impact of teen-oriented pop music in the mid-1960s."

On the show, Bernstein reserves his greatest praise for the "5 percent" of these pop musicians whom he regards as "formidable." Included among them are the Beatles, Brian Wilson, and, not surprisingly, Simon and Garfunkel. The accidental success of their first number-one hit single, "The Sound of Silence," gave them the confidence and the clout to develop their unique vision of what singers and songwriters could accomplish artistically within the framework of rock and roll and contemporary popular music. The progression from *Wednesday Morning, 3 A.M.* to *The Sounds of Silence* to *Parsley, Sage, Rosemary and Thyme* definitely made them contenders in the "rock album as art" sweepstakes. Like the cream of the crop of their contemporaries, Paul and Art were not only positioned, but also *expected* to unleash something unique, explosive, and groundbreaking in 1967.

Unfortunately, the writer for the duo, Paul, hit a dry spell. This was a time in the record business when artists were contractually obligated to release at least two and sometimes three full albums in a calendar year. The Beatles did it. The Beach Boys did it. And so did Bob Dylan. The fact that Simon and Garfunkel went albumless for a whole year (and then some) was definitely a source of concern for the executives at Columbia Records, who demanded "product" from their primary "capital generators" to keep the coffers brimming with the increasingly vast amount of discretionary income that consumers were willing to spend on their favorite recording artists.

Paul and Art were not completely dormant in '67. Far from it. In addition to "At the Zoo," there was a full slate of concert appearances. They also participated as organizers of and performers at the fabled Monterey International Pop Festival in June. Simon knew what he had to do next, what he had to accomplish. He told *High Fidelity* magazine in 1967, "I'm not interested in singles anymore. Besides, I work very hard on my songs. They come slowly." *Hit Parader* magazine was a little harsher in its assessment of the situation:

> The word blight or whatever it was which afflicted Bob Dylan for more than a year claimed another significant victim for a roughly concurrent 18 months: Paul Simon, the writing half of Simon and Garfunkel . . . *Bookends* was started early in 1967 but Simon, who makes his living by being sensitive, suddenly became so sensitive that he was unable to write, a problem which was not resolved until this year.

And *that* was the cause of great concern in the executive suites at Columbia Records.

In fact, it was the cause of so much concern that Columbia president Clive Davis assigned a staff producer to jump-start the recording of a new album by Art and Paul. That person would go on to become one of the most artistically and commercially successful record producers of the late sixties and beyond. A list of his credits reads like a who's who of great rock-and-roll performers: Janis Joplin; Leonard Cohen; Blood, Sweat and Tears; and the Band among them. His name is John Simon (no relation to Paul), and his first taste of success in the rock arena was as producer, for a group called the Cyrkle, of a number-two hit single, "Red Rubber Ball," which, of course, was written by Paul Simon and Bruce Woodley of the Seekers in 1964.

John described what happened to him after that: "I used to be in a 10-by-10, windowless office as an associate producer. After the Cyrkle record was a hit, they gave me an office that was much bigger, with a window and a plant! They also gave me artists to record like Leonard Cohen and Simon and Garfunkel—artists who had some kind of track record. They assigned Simon and Garfunkel to me because they were having trouble getting a new album out of them . . . According to Clive Davis, they were dragging their feet. That album eventually became *Bookends*, though it took so long to do that I eventually left Columbia Records in the middle of that album."

John is what you might call a real artist's producer. He quickly bonded with Art and Paul and tells a great story about their relationship with the "suits" at the record company: "Clive Davis was a lawyer. When I met him, he was one of four or five lawyers on staff at Columbia. Then he became president of the label. I think he thought that just by taking Paul and Art into his office and having a fatherly talk with them, he could get them to move along on this album and speed things up a little bit. What he didn't know was that they took a tape recorder in with them to this meeting and—I don't know if he knows it to this day—made a tape of Clive trying to convince them that they should go ahead and make an album. I haven't heard this tape in years, so I couldn't begin to quote it. All I know is that we got a pretty good laugh out of it!"

John spoke recently about the genesis and nature of his working relationship with Art and Paul: "My first session with them was to do a song called 'Fakin' It' [in June 1967]. They were signed [to Columbia] as a duo, a folk duo, and they were signed under an old contract that specified that the record company would pay the recording costs. [This was] because the company assumed that as a folk duo, how much could the recording costs be? Nothing. So here they have this contract that says that the record company will pay for everything they do in the studio. So what do they do? They take advantage of it, of course. Paul and Artie said, 'We want this to have strings on it, but we want it to be lower strings and a little bit mellower than violins.' So I said, 'Okay, we will get muted violas.' 'Then we want brass to do some little punctuations.' 'Okay.' 'Then we want some percussion to come in.' 'Okay.'

"I'm an arranger as well as a producer, so I basically took dictation from them about what they wanted. I fleshed it out a little bit, wrote the arrangements out, and booked string players to come in for an hour because this was a pretty simple chart they had in mind. Then the second hour would be brass players. Then the third hour would be percussionists. And this was a very simple thing they had in mind.

"Well, there we are, and the eight viola players show up in the studio and they're all calling their answering services because there have never been eight violas without violins or cellos in a session that they could recall. They all thought they were in the wrong place! We got started and we played the chart down, and Artie and Paul were in the control room. After we finished playing their part down once, they started tuning up a little bit. And the talk-back button came on and a voice said, 'What was that? What was that?' And I said, 'What was what?' And they said, 'That sound just then. What was that?' I said, 'Well, they're just tuning up to the track and each other.' 'We like that! That's great! Forget the chart. Let's do that! Let's do that!'

"We ended up spending—gee, I don't know how long—*hours* trying to get that random sound of them tuning up. Paul and Artie didn't care because they weren't paying for it. Columbia was paying for the studio time. Meanwhile, the brass players were out in the hall backing up. They didn't care because they were going to get over-time. And behind them, the percussion players were backing up, and this 3-hour session went on all night long! Eventually, I don't know how many of these fragments came out on the song in the end."

Art chalks this up to the atmospheric conditions of the era: "Being in the studio and making records in the sixties, I can tell you, it was very uncorporate. It was highly spirited. It was kids at play. It was just a wonder that you were allowed to do this, that two middle-class kids can sign a contract, rehearse and get their talent into the studio, and then find that the entire distribution network is waiting to put out their products. It was wonderfully simple, sincere, and uncynical."

"Fakin' It" came out in July 1967, smack in the middle of the heralded Summer of Love. It has been said that there were three unquestionably essential long-playing albums that season: *Sgt. Pepper*, of course, *Surrealistic Pillow* by the Jefferson Airplane, and the debut album by the Doors. Had they been able to pull it off, it's not hard to imagine a new album from Simon and Garfunkel being on that list as well. But the synergy of the *Graduate* soundtrack and *Bookends* was still almost a year away, so their fans had to settle for "Fakin' It" to glean some clues about what Simon and Garfunkel were up to. They weren't disappointed.

The single was only a modest success, but it kept Simon and Garfunkel on AM radio that summer. Far more important were the new FM rock radio stations that played album cuts instead of just singles and treated the new music with seriousness and respect. That is where Art and Paul found a true home for their work. In terms of airplay and reverence, their catalog of recordings stood shoulder to shoulder with the holy trinity of sixties rock and roll: the Beatles, the Stones, and Bob Dylan.

In addition to "Fakin' It," John Simon's work with Art and Paul included the album tracks "Punky's Dilemma," "Save the Life of My Child," and "Overs," all of which ultimately found their way onto *Bookends*. Each was marked with an asterisk crediting John for "production assistance." Here's another example of what that work entailed. During the first week of October 1967, Art, Paul, John Simon, Roy Halee, and an assistant engineer went into Columbia's recording studio on 52nd Street in New York City to work on "Punky's Dilemma." As luck would have it, musician and writer Morgan Ames was a fly on the wall at one of those sessions and wrote an article about what went on that night for the November 1967 issue of *High Fidelity* magazine. Ames's ear and eyewitness glimpses caught the following snapshots of the track in progress:

Finally work begins . . . The track is made in layers. First Simon's guitar, then his voice. Later he'll repeat his vocal line, overdubbing it to add body . . . After the take, Garfunkel flips the intercom switch connected to a speaker in the studio. "Try it again, Paul. I think your feeling was a little better the last time. But your intonation is fine now." . . . The team's working relationship is built upon listening to each other, asking advice, taking it, building each other's morale. Though it's obvious they enjoy working with John Simon, the last word seems to come from one partner to the other . . . The skeletal guitar track is played over and over. Producer John Simon adds some chords played on a toy piano, the kind sold in variety stores. Whistling is added, then finger-snapping . . . Work continues slowly. Simon wants more nonmusical sounds dotted into the track, "personality fills." Simon, Garfunkel, John Simon, and Roy Halee go into the studio and the search for usable objects begins . . . Ideas are tried, accepted, rejected. Time passes. Too much time. Too little headway . . . "Punky's Dilemma" is put aside for the moment and Simon begins work on the title song for the new album, "Bookends."

Between the Ames article and John Simon's recollection recounted earlier, it's easy to see why *Bookends* was a year and a half in the making. That brings up the question of perfectionism. Was it Paul? Was it Artie? Was it Roy Halee? When Paul Zollo asked Paul about this in an interview for his book *Songwriters on Songwriting*, Paul had a ready answer:

> No. It isn't perfectionism. It was waiting for the thing to come alive. I would say, actually, I'm a little sloppy. The perfectionists are really Roy Halee and Art Garfunkel. Those guys are much more perfectionists. They would really stay on one detail. Whereas if I see what it's supposed to be, that's enough for me. I'm ready to move on. Whereas they want to get the fine shading right.

Perfectionism or no perfectionism, slump or no slump, *Sgt. Pepper* or no *Sgt. Pepper*, what's closer to the truth is that Simon and Garfunkel could afford to slow down the frantic pace of the recording process a little bit. They were a hot commodity. They sold lots of records. They had amassed a large and loyal following that would go to see them in concert wherever and whenever they chose to perform.

One of those concerts brought them to Fordham University in New York City in October 1967. The pop-music world was still very much under the spell of *Sgt. Pepper*, which had been released the previous June. Almost a year had passed since *Parsley, Sage, Rosemary and Thyme*, and *Bookends* was still 6 months away. Paul was asked if part of the reason for the long delay was that the duo was feeling some pressure because of what Brian Wilson had done

68

with *Pet Sounds* and the Beatles with *Sgt. Pepper*. He answered not boastfully, but quite matter-of-factly, "When we finished *Parsley, Sage*, we were already way past *Parsley, Sage*, and the level I envisioned that we would be on, I hadn't written yet. I just saw it. I just said, 'Well, we have to do it this way.' It took a long time to get there really. First, I had to change my writing style. It's really quite different now from 'Dangling Conversation'— that's an older style. The new stuff is not really like that musically. So that took time. Then, there's the normal pressures. And, of course, the Beatles album was a big spur to everybody. They really showed that you can do a tremendous amount in an album. I always knew that you could, but here they were, and they did it! I figured that we were gonna be the first ones to do that—not the electronic stuff, but to make an album that was a total album. They came out and they beat us to it, they beat us to the punch. I was half disappointed and I was half glad because it was a great album. I listen to it all the time. That was the extent of the pressure. I knew that there were other people who were more talented and were doing things that . . . took the wind out of me at first. But you bounce back."

Twenty years later, when I suggested to him that he and Artie were peers of the Beatles, he said, "Yes, we are peers in that we all are about the same age, but the Beatles happened earlier. The Beatles, Stones, and Dylan all happened a year or two earlier than Simon and Garfunkel.

1967

They were there first and it just remained that way. Those were the first three big superstars of the new sixties movement, and we came just a half step behind it. I don't mean to imply that I would have done as good a piece of work as *Sgt. Pepper's Lonely Hearts Club Band,* because that is *the* album of the sixties, I think. But we were fooling around with different studio techniques and different ideas of expanding records, so I was really surprised when that record came out and they were there. Not only were they there, but they were way better than I was going to be anyway."

During the Fordham interview, Art Garfunkel was even more expansive than his partner in his description of what the duo had up their sleeves for the next project: "Paul slowed down his speed in writing. It's been a little tougher this year than it was last year because there's a lot of things to do. It's sort of a slump. He's coming out of it now. We really can't record until the songs are ready. We've planned the album and we know what it's going to be. We knew a year ago as soon as we finished *Parsley, Sage.* We went to work on it, but always in a planning stage. It's only in the last 2 months that we've gotten busy recording all the ideas. I think now it will be another month and it will be out in December." He was off by 5 months.

Garfunkel continued: "It's very gratifying to put something into words, say something, and know that it's going to go onto thousands of radios and reach millions of people. That's a tremendous source of power. It's like a waiting audience that has ears and minds that want to think. And with that waiting audience, you don't want to just fool around.

"We would like to treat the record and the fact that you pick up your needle and put it on something and that it stays there for a half an hour and sound comes out—treat it in the broadest possible sense. In other words, working with that fact and tearing down every other written law which usually goes with that, we would like to do an awful lot of experimentation. The idea of juxtaposing themes. The idea of stopping songs in the middle. Just the fact that you're working with sound—as long as you accept just that and don't write any more rules into the game. Leave yourself very, very free. There's a tremendous amount still to be done that groups haven't done yet."

Paul added, "I'm gonna work with various levels of consciousness in records. In '7 o'Clock News/Silent Night,' you have somebody talking and somebody singing, and the listener mixes them in his mind and gets an impression from the two things. But I think you could do it with maybe three or four things at one time, and that way, you can give 'em . . . you can color your pictures with more skill. I can take a situation and show it from four different angles at the same time. [It would] be closer to life. Closer to the way things are. You don't catch everything that's going on. I can hear this voice vaguely

1967

over there, but I don't know what he's saying. It's just an impression. Well, that's what I want to do on records."

The stage was set. The appetite was whetted. Brian Wilson, the mad genius from Hawthorne, California, had laid down the gauntlet in 1966; the royal princes of the British Invasion had raised the bar to dizzying heights in 1967. Now, it was almost time to find out what the intellectual dynamic duo from Queens, New York, would do to push the creative envelope even further. But I don't think anyone expected or was quite prepared for the dramatic rise in popularity that Art and Paul were about to experience thanks to a motion picture that would take the country by storm.

6

THE GRADUATE

As the calendar began running out on 1967, another blast of good timing and good fortune catapulted Simon and Garfunkel to an even greater level of fame and influence. That blast came from another very powerful form of mass communications. The cultural sensibility of the 1960s was most evident in the popular music of that decade. Rock stars stole some of the thunder from movie stars, but a few extraordinary films reflected with aching accuracy the undercurrents that were causing a seismic shift in the landscape of American society. The film industry was forced to adapt to a changing culture, a changing audience, a changing business, and a changing world. A number of exceptional movies fueled the fire and fanned the flames that year, and many of them had rock-and-roll soundtracks.

The power and popularity of rock and roll as the soundtrack of a movie was nothing new. It began in the fifties, when film director Richard Brooks used "Rock

Around the Clock" by Bill Haley and the Comets during the opening credits of *Blackboard Jungle*. The song had been released a year before and gone nowhere. But the synergy between music and the movies propelled it onto the charts, where it became the first rock-and-roll national number-one record and essentially launched what has come to be known as the rock era. The trend continued with Elvis Presley a year later. Legendary disc jockey Alan Freed made a series of low-budget, high-profit movies featuring a roster of top-shelf rock-and-roll talent. Even established movie icons such as Bing Crosby and John Wayne realized the value of using so-called "teen idols" in their films to attract a younger audience. It worked. Wayne, in particular, made a habit of it, enlisting teen heartthrob Fabian for *North to Alaska*, Frankie Avalon for *The Alamo*, and Ricky Nelson for *Rio Bravo*.

Artists such as the late Gene Pitney scored huge hits with the title songs of *Town Without Pity* and *The Man Who Shot Liberty Valance*. The Beatles made a triumphant entry into feature films with their critically acclaimed debut, *A Hard Day's Night*. The floodgates opened. The Byrds did the title song for a Tony Curtis movie called *Don't Make Waves*. The Turtles did the same for *A Guide for the Married Man*. The Supremes sang the title song for *The Happening*. The Lovin' Spoonful's music appeared in Woody Allen's *What's Up, Tiger Lily* and Francis Ford Coppola's early movie *You're a Big Boy*

Now. But the best example of rock being used on a film soundtrack happened in 1967, when esteemed director Mike Nichols chose Simon and Garfunkel to do the music for a film he was working on. Nichols had been half of the acclaimed comedy team Nichols and May (with Elaine May). When they went their separate ways, Nichols became a film director, and his debut effort was the award-winning *Who's Afraid of Virginia Woolf*, starring Richard Burton and Elizabeth Taylor.

The genesis of Nichols's new project was a novel published in 1963 by Charles Webb. It was about a newly minted college graduate with a severe case of high anxiety about his personal and professional future. It was called *The Graduate*. Hollywood producer Lawrence Turman read about it in the *New York Times* and decided that it could be the basis for a very interesting feature-length motion picture. He enlisted Nichols to sculpt the story for the big screen. Nichols told the *Directors Guild of America Monthly* in their January 2004 issue that he was halfway through shooting the film, when his brother sent him *Parsley, Sage, Rosemary and Thyme*. He played the album continuously for 4 weeks. "In the middle of the fourth week," he said, "I'm listening to a great score! This is the score! We started putting it in then and there while we were still shooting. And then I met Simon and Garfunkel, and they were quite uninterested in the whole thing. They said, 'Oh OK. Well, yes, it's alright, you can use it.' They were very blasé."

In the May 15, 2005, issue of *Variety*, Peter Bart wrote:

Nichols had become obsessed with Simon and Garfunkel's music while shooting the film. Lawrence Turman, his producer, made a deal for Simon to write three new songs for the movie. By the time they were nearly finished editing the film, Simon had only written one new song ["Punky's Dilemma," for the scene in which Dustin Hoffman's character floats aimlessly in his parents' backyard pool. The song never made it into the film]. Nichols begged him for more but Simon, who was touring constantly, told him he didn't have the time. He did play for him a few notes of a new song he had been working on; "It's not for the movie . . . it's a song about times past—about Mrs. Roosevelt and Joe DiMaggio and stuff." Nichols advised Simon, "It's now about Mrs. Robinson, not Mrs. Roosevelt."

In the end, Nichols decided to go with previously released Simon and Garfunkel recordings. "Punky's Dilemma" and "Overs" were cast aside in favor of "The Sound of Silence," "April Come She Will," "The Big Bright Green Pleasure Machine," and "Scarborough Fair/ Canticle." The only new Paul Simon material in the film was a couple of snippets of the chorus of the song now known as "Mrs. Robinson." (Paul hadn't written the verses yet.)

The Graduate premiered on December 21, 1967, in New York City. The film caught lightning in a bottle. One of the major components of its success was generational. What had been previously described as a generation gap was really more like a generation chasm. You could sum it up with opposing slogans: "My Country, Right or Wrong!"; "Hell No, We Won't Go!"; "America: Love It or Leave It!"; "Hey! Hey! LBJ, How Many Kids Did You Kill Today?"; "The Middle Finger"; "The Peace Sign"; and so on. The antiwar demonstrations, the civil rights movement, the sexual revolution, the burgeoning drug culture, and the nascent rise of women's liberation all served to polarize the nation. At the core of these divisions was a sea change in the shifting values of the older and younger generations.

Peter Biskind, in his book *Easy Riders, Raging Bulls: How the Sex-Drugs-and-Rock 'n' Roll Generation Saved Hollywood*, claims that audiences were ready for a more challenging cinema like *The Graduate*: "You had the generation gap, [with] Abbie Hoffman saying, 'Don't trust anyone over 30.' The famous word 'plastics' encapsulates the theme of the movie, which is that the adult world is artificial, is superficial, on some level immoral and irrelevant to the concerns of young people."

So many elements were crucial to the success of *The*

Graduate. One was the dream cast, beginning first and foremost with the career-launching debut performance by Dustin Hoffman as the title character, along with Anne Bancroft's bravura turn as Mrs. Robinson and stellar support from veteran actors such as William Daniels, Murray Hamilton, and Norman Fell. Another was the delicious screenplay by Calder Willingham and Buck Henry. And, of course, the music of Simon and Garfunkel supplied the perfect tone for both the comedic content of the film and its more serious and introspective aspects.

It was the highest grossing film of 1968 and received seven Academy Award nominations. It ranked number seven on the American Film Institute's list of the greatest films of the century. And it raised the bar for movie soundtracks by using contemporary music to sell albums and bring viewers to the movies, a practice that has grown exponentially in the 4 decades since. Of course, it also raised Simon and Garfunkel's profile in an explosive, dynamic fashion. Art describes the elevator ride to the top:

> I remember having lived through it, and I saw the levels of popularity that I thought we had reached with the public, and I saw it expand. Our first hit, 'The Sound of Silence,' was [at] the end of 1965. We soon got a manager, Mort Lewis, and soon began to do college concerts. So by 1966, we were touring artists with our second and third follow-up

hit singles. We then put out an album late in 1966, *Parsley, Sage, Rosemary and Thyme*, which, like the Beatles', was one of those more 'arty' albums. So, like the Beatles, we were expanding the notion of what a record album could be, and that was an exciting aspect of who Simon and Garfunkel were. And I remember feeling that gave us a certain dimension with the public. We couldn't just make pop singles, but we could make albums with conceptual [ideas]. We started making richer albums and we were touring.

Then in 1967 came Mike Nichols's movie *The Graduate* with Dustin Hoffman, and the use of 'The Sound of Silence' and 'Scarborough Fair/Canticle' almost doubled our popularity. That's what I felt.

It also did something else. It set up the record-buying public perfectly for the release of both the soundtrack album for *The Graduate* and the long-awaited album of all-new material from Simon and Garfunkel.

As usual, there were tension and dissension along the way. Clive Davis had purchased the rights to release the soundtrack on Columbia, thinking that it would contain a healthy number of new Simon and Garfunkel songs. When that turned out not to be the case, all he was left with were two snippets of "Mrs. Robinson" and a handful of previously released songs. After seeing the film, Davis realized he could fill out the soundtrack with the semi-satirical music composed for the film by David Grusin. The Simon and Garfunkel camp was aghast at the idea. They were much more concerned about finishing *Bookends* and devoting all their energies to making it a success. But Davis promised to release the recordings in tandem, and that the resulting synergy would stimulate the sales of both. Art and Paul reluctantly agreed and got back to work on their "other" project for 1968.

1968

Artistic endeavors do not become successful in a vacuum. They play out against a backdrop of all kinds of cultural, political, and social upheaval. Hit movies, stage plays, books, television shows, and musical recordings very often (intentionally or unintentionally) tap into the undercurrents at play at any given moment in human history. How else to explain the enormous success of *The Graduate* or, for that matter, *Bookends* itself?

Work on *Bookends* was finally coming to an end. After John Simon's departure from Columbia Records at the end of 1967, it became clear that Paul, Art, and Roy Halee would complete production themselves. On February 1, "America" was recorded. On February 2, the final version of "Mrs. Robinson" was recorded. And, finally, "Old Friends" and the closing "Bookends Theme" were recorded on March 8.

Bookends cannot be separated from the tumultuous events of 1968 for a number of reasons. First and foremost is the fact that the album was released on April 3, 1968, exactly 1 day before the mind-numbing assassination of the Reverend Doctor Martin Luther King Jr. in Memphis, Tennessee. This coincidence alone lent gravitas to the major themes and, in some cases, the actual songs and lyrics on *Bookends*: "I'm empty and aching and I don't know why"; "Where have you gone, Joe DiMaggio? A nation turns its lonely eyes to you"; "Oh, my Grace, I got no hiding place"; "I have a photograph / Preserve your memories, they're all that's left you." How many events from 1968 could those sentiments be applied to? Take your pick:

The capture of the *U.S.S. Pueblo* by the North Koreans

Senator Eugene McCarthy's "Clean for Gene" Democratic presidential candidacy

Senator Robert F. Kennedy's entry into the presidential race on St. Patrick's Day

President Lyndon Johnson's stunning announcement that he wouldn't seek another term

Race riots and demonstrations at universities across the country

Senator Robert Kennedy's senseless assassination in June ("Mrs. Robinson" was the number-one single in America the day Kennedy was killed)

Antiwar protests and police brutality at the Democratic Convention in Chicago in August

The election of Richard M. Nixon in November

For many who experienced these events firsthand, *Bookends* served as a kind of comfort food—a security blanket to wrap yourself up in when the local, national, or international news became too much to bear. And the music it contained seemed somewhat chameleon-like in the sense that the more upbeat songs could distract you from the chaos going on in the world, while the more serious tracks were perfectly in tune with the somber, contemplative, and reflective emotions that you were also unavoidably experiencing. Four decades later, it can still evoke those very strong feelings in many, including myself, who consider it to be a singular work, one of the greatest popular-music albums ever made.

It's time to "listen" to *Bookends*.

7

BOOKENDS

SIDE ONE

One of the great pleasures of purchasing a long-playing album in the 1960s was the moment when it first came into your possession. What does the cover look like? Are the lyrics printed on the sleeve? Are there liner notes that will tell you something revealing about the musicians or the music within? You could hold it in your hands, and you didn't need reading glasses or bifocals or a magnifying glass to decipher the printing.

Four decades ago, album covers became almost as important as the music itself. When rock and roll took over as the primary engine driving the recording industry, album covers became more and more elaborate and artistic. Major figures from the art world were sought out to design, draw, or paint cover artwork. Andy Warhol created packages for the Velvet Underground and, later, the Rolling Stones (*Sticky Fingers*, complete with a working zipper on the front!). Even the venerable Norman Rockwell did an original painting for *The Live Adventures of Al Kooper and Mike Bloomfield*. Johnny Carson wrote liner notes for Kenny Rankin, and Bill Cosby did the same for the Temptations. As usual, the Beatles set a high standard with the packaging of *Sgt. Pepper's Lonely Hearts Club Band*. The Stones followed their lead with a "moving picture illusion" on the cover of *Their Satanic Majesties Request*. Psychedelic colors and graphics were the order of the day.

Simon and Garfunkel? As always, they marched to the beat of a different drummer. The other concept albums were bathed in every shade of the rainbow. *Bookends* was not. As we pointed out in Chapter 1, it was black and white and gray—telegraphing many of the moods of the music and lyrics of the songs. Richard Avedon, one of the best photographers in the world, was commissioned to do the stark, up-close, in-your-face portrait that adorns the cover. During one interview, Artie was shown all of the Simon and Garfunkel album covers to get his off-the-cuff impressions of them. When he got to *Bookends*, he immediately smiled, pointed to Paul on the cover, and said, "There's Richard Avedon reflected in the irises of Paul's eyes!" Take a look for yourself, but you'll have to use a 12-inch vinyl copy of the record. On a CD copy, the shrunken, telescoped image is virtually impossible to see.

Side one of *Bookends* is the heart and soul of the project. In consort with Roy Halee (and, to a lesser extent, John Simon), Art and Paul at this time truly came into their own as the producers of their own music and albums.

All the talking and thinking and planning since *Parsley, Sage, Rosemary and Thyme* finally came to fruition on this album. Instead of a string of unrelated songs, side one is a fully conceived and executed concept. It is a suite of songs and melodies about the life cycle, from birth to death, from womb to tomb, from innocence through disillusionment to resignation. Many of Paul's major and recurring themes are given free rein here: alienation, desperation, friendship, loneliness, mortality, and relationships.

The subject matter of *Bookends* is, at one and the same time, very personal and specific, yet very universal and general. The juxtapositions that defined 1968 were jarring: hawk versus dove, black versus white, love versus hate, life versus death, even acoustic versus electric. All these disparate elements found their way into the grooves of the *Bookends* suite—maybe not overtly, maybe not even consciously, but they're all there. You can hear it for yourself 32 seconds into the album, when the wistful, ethereal, acoustic "Bookends Theme" shifts gears and revs up right into the searing, ominous chords that launch "Save the Life of My Child." Any notion that this recording would be business as usual or "Scarborough Fair" revisited were put to rest by the desperate tableau about the suicidal boy getting ready to jump from the ledge.

"Save the Life of My Child" is probably the first example of "sampling" used in a popular-music recording. This practice became widespread in hip-hop and is now an influential part of American musical culture. Typically, a rhythmic musical phrase is taken from an older hit and looped repetitively on the new track. Many of these recordings are quite different from the type of music usually associated with Simon and Garfunkel. While no one would ever mistake Snoop Doggy Dogg for Paul or Sean "Diddy" Combs for Artie, the simple truth is that all four men used sampling for dramatic emphasis. "Save the Life of My Child" samples "The Sound of Silence" to illustrate and heighten for the listener the sense of despair felt by the young man on the ledge: "Hello, darkness, my old friend . . . "

Art told me about another innovation in the song: "I remember we were touring when Paul said, 'I'm going to start writing now a whole side of an album—a cycle of songs. I want the early ones to be about youth and the last song to be about old age, and I want the feel of each song to fit.' So, it starts off [after 'Bookends Theme'] with 'Save the Life of My Child.' A kid's gonna jump off a building. It's the first use of the synthesizer, I think, [on a record]. It had just been invented. We were taking courses in what the sawtooth wave was all about. It has a synthesized bass in it, which I believe is the first use of synthesizer on anybody's record."

John Simon (who is credited for production assistance on the track) corroborated Artie's recollection. "I was learning on the job and so were they. We had Bob Moog, who had invented the Moog synthesizer, the first model of which was as big as a small car. So on "Save the Life of My Child," the bass line is me playing the Moog synthesizer, and Bob Moog was in the studio showing us how to get these sounds and things."

Perhaps it is the synthesizer that gives the track its dark, palpable feeling of horror. It jumps out of the speakers at you. Wasting no time at all, Simon sets the scene. Coming fast and furious is a whole set of images: a boy on a ledge about to jump, an elderly man fainting, a desperate mother screaming out the title's words. There's a woman calling the cops, a supposition about drug use, a disgruntled Officer MacDougal. Simon even squeezes in a sly comment about the contrast in the editorial approaches of New York's two leading newspapers, the *Times* and the *Daily News*. Finally, night falls, a spotlight hits the boy, and he jumps, intoning the despairing phrase, "Oh, my Grace, I got no hiding place."

The lyrics alone convey the chaos and confusion of the incident, but it's the sounds that Art, Paul, Roy, and John created in the studio that underscore the tragedy. They are using the studio as a kind of super-instrument, much like the Beatles did throughout *Sgt. Pepper's Lonely Hearts Club Band*. The track is a virtual sound collage. The voices screaming in the background give you the feeling that you're listening to a chorus from the bowels of hell. "Bookends Theme" is comparable to the first, gentle ascent of a roller coaster on its way up that first rise, but then—look out! All hell breaks loose as the coaster plummets. "Save the Life of My Child" is definitely the beginning of the roller coaster ride that is side one of *Bookends*.

Then what? A slow fade on the "Oh, my Grace" line blends seamlessly into the soft, humming harmony that starts off one of Paul's greatest writing achievements in this phase of his career—"America." In a review of *Simon and Garfunkel's Greatest Hits* in *Rolling Stone* magazine, *New York Times* critic Stephen Holden wrote:

> "America," from the *Bookends* album, was Simon's next major step forward. It is three and a half minutes of sheer brilliance, whose unforced narrative, alternating precise detail with sweeping observation, evokes the panorama of restless, paved America, and simultaneously illuminates a drama of shared loneliness on a bus trip with cosmic implications.

Garfunkel says that "America" is about "young lovers with their adventure and optimism," and, yes, it does start out that way, but by the end, a whole other mood has been introduced into the mix. On a bus, with the young woman next to him asleep, the narrator exclaims painfully to no one in particular, "I'm empty and aching and I don't know why." Then, shifting immediately from the personal to the universal, Paul invokes a metaphor of counting automobiles on the New Jersey Turnpike to remind us of all the lost souls wandering the highways and byways of mid-sixties America, struggling to navigate the rapids between despair and hope, optimism and disillusionment. This song has always brought to my mind the final scene in *The Graduate*. Benjamin and Elaine (in her bridal gown) are sitting at the back of the bus following Ben's outrageous disruption of Elaine's wedding to another man. Heart-pumping exhilaration is quickly replaced by confusion and fear, with their straight-ahead, blank stares showing their thoughts: "What now? What the hell happens next?" That last shot sabotages the conventional "happy ending" of a Hollywood movie.

The film's director, Mike Nichols, said in *Director's Guild of America Monthly* that the final scene was a happy accident. "On the day we shot the scene," Nichols explained,

> I said to Dustin [Hoffman] and Katharine [Ross], "Look, we've stopped traffic for miles and we have a police escort and I cannot do this over and over and over. So please, just get on the bus and laugh, OK?" And they looked at me terrified, and I thought, "What am I doing? Am I nuts? I'm just scaring them to death." But it was too late, and they

got on the bus and they tried to laugh. They looked very unhappy and terrified because I had terrified them. The next day I saw the dailies, and I thought, "Look at this. It's the end of the movie!" Some part of me knew better than I did.

Consciously or not, Paul Simon captures the exact same ambivalence in "America."

After the bus disappears down the turnpike and "America" begins its long, slow instrumental fadeout, we are greeted by a familiar and easily identifiable series of sounds—the striking of a match, the lighting of a cigarette, and a deep inhalation and exhalation of smoke by a man who seems to be carrying the weight of the world on his shoulders. (Today, the use of a cigarette is politically incorrect, but this was 1968—3 years after the Surgeon General's first warnings about smoking's effects on health and 2 years before tobacco advertising was banned on American radio and television.) Next we hear a softly played acoustic guitar and a mournful Paul Simon singing a solo lead vocal part about a disintegrating relationship. No Garfunkel yet, but that's just setting up one of the greatest vocal overlaps in Simon and Garfunkel's recorded history. As Paul laments the passing of joy from the relationship, he ends the thought with the word *time*. At that precise moment, Artie's angelic voice sweeps in with another observation that begins with the same word. It is seamless, flawless, and beautiful. Artie says of that transition: "'Overs' is more of an older couple beginning to tire of each other—'Time is tapping on my forehead, hanging from my mirror, rattling the teacups.' These are good words. [Paul's] a good writer."

There is terrific wordplay with the multiple meanings of the word *over* right up to the last line of the song, when the protagonist is mulling over the idea of leaving, but stops to "think it over." Is this another nod to *The Graduate*, with its depiction of a couple in a loveless marriage (the Robinsons) staying together out of habit more than anything else?

The song ends with the spoken word *over* hanging in the air. It is followed in short order by another 2:06 sound collage titled "Voices of Old People." The credit reads, "Art Garfunkel recorded old people in various locations in New York and Los Angeles over a period of several months. These voices were taken from those tapes. We wish to thank the United Home for Aged Hebrews and the California Home for the Aged at Reseda for their cooperation." Art says simply, "I recorded old people as a setup to the song 'Old Friends.' I wanted the sound of their voices to set up the texture of the song."

For Art, capturing the wheezes, coughs, sighs, and earthy sounds from the backs of the throats of the old people was just as important as what they were saying. The sentiments expressed by these men and women near the end of their lives were emotional and moving, and they remain so 4 decades later. And, yes, they provided the *perfect* setup for what followed: the old-age section of the song cycle, in which Paul imagines two elderly gentlemen sharing a park bench at the age of 70.

There are two great media moments about aging in rock and roll. One already happened, when Paul McCartney turned 64 on June 21, 2006. Who would have believed that the age cited in the song he wrote for *Sgt. Pepper's Lonely Hearts Club Band* called "When I'm 64" could come to pass so quickly? As of this writing, the second milestone has not yet occurred. After November 4, 2011, Paul Simon and Art Garfunkel will both be 70 years of age. "Old Friends" is a song and a phrase that will always be associated with Simon and Garfunkel (even during those times when they are not being too friendly with one another). Paul's 20-something extrapolation of aging was affecting when it first came out, and it becomes only more touching and resonant as the real people come closer to synching up with the characters on the park bench. Artie was once asked if he and Paul were aware back then that they would one day fill those roles. He answered, "Yeah. We're such old, deep friends, Paul and I. From junior high school, the notion that we possibly would go through life together as old friends came to us very early. And here we are years later. We are friends and we always will be. I think we knew we were talking about ourselves as old friends."

When the interviewer joked to Art that there would probably be a cable special when the events described in the song came to pass, Art took on the persona of a director, yelling, "Somebody bring in the newspaper. Now blow it in the grass. Boys, you're not wearing those round toes!" Even Paul, who tends to be dismissive of a lot of his early work, has a warm spot in his heart for both that song and the album. He's been quoted as saying that he feels *Bookends* is "the quintessential Simon and Garfunkel album."

———

Now where are we in the song cycle? The roller coaster ride is nearly at an end, but wait a minute. What's this? The soft notes of "Bookends Theme" are back, bringing side one full circle. Only this time, there are lyrics that speak about time passed, innocence, confidences, and saving photographs to preserve memories. The life journey has come full circle, and there's still all of side two to discover, savor, and digest.

SIDE TWO

If ever a vinyl album has suffered by being transferred from analog to digital technology, from vinyl album to compact disc, it is *Bookends*. Why? Simple: CDs do not have a side one and a side two. They offer a continuous stream of music from the first track to the last. But that isn't the way older albums were conceived, that isn't the

———

way they were constructed, and that isn't the way they were meant to be listened to. These truths have been lost on the CD version of *Bookends*, and that's too bad because side one was meant to be heard as a piece. It was meant to be listened to as a layered, structured whole unto itself. It was meant to be absorbed, reflected upon, talked about, and appreciated. The audience was expected to pause for a few moments as the final note of "Bookends Theme" evaporated into thin air.

Then, after taking a short interval to think about it, the listener was expected to grab the record at its edge with both hands (carefully, mind you, so as not to scratch or smudge the vinyl) and flip it over on the turntable to await the pleasures of side two. Not unfamiliar pleasures, like those in the new songs on side one, but rather the familiar pleasures of songs previously released only as 45 rpm singles.

The lead track was "Fakin' It." As mentioned earlier, it was the first song that John Simon had produced for the duo after Clive Davis had assigned him to get them moving on a new album of original material. Simon was in a unique position. On the one hand, he was the "suit" brought in by the powers that be to protect their investment; on the other hand, he was a young man who also loved art and music and bonded immediately with the artists he was to produce.

"Fakin' It" furthered Art and Paul's mission to expand the possibilities of popular-music recordings. It opens and closes with an unearthly rhythmic sound created in the studio (which some critics have said owes a huge debt to "Strawberry Fields" by the Beatles). It walks a tight-rope between electric and acoustic instruments. It has dramatic tempo changes. And it plants in the middle of the recording a spoken-word vignette featuring a woman with a British accent entering a tailor shop and greeting the proprietor with the words "Good morning, Mr. Leitch. Have you had a busy day?"

Paul has said that the idea for the vignette came from musing about where he would have lived and what he would have done if he had been born a hundred years ear-lier. His first assumption was that he would have been where his ancestors came from—Vienna or Hungary. Then he tried to figure out what he might have done for a living for the line in "Fakin' It" where he speculates about an occupation. His first thought was that he would have been a sailor, but he quickly rejected that. He then began to imagine that a more likely profession for him a hun-dred years before might have been as a tailor, and that's what he went with for the final recording. The young British woman on the track was a singer named Beverly Martyn, who was friendly with singer–songwriter Dono-van. Donovan's last name was Leitch, so that name was used in the spoken-word part of the song.

Sometime after this song was written, Paul's father told him that his father—Paul's grandfather—who had died when Paul was very young, had also been named Paul

Simon and was a tailor from Vienna! Naturally, Paul was blown away by the coincidence. It was sixties serendipity at its finest!

———

Next up on side two is the delightful "Punky's Dilemma," a piece of Paul Simon whimsy that showcases his great facility with wordplay, his cleverness, and his not so often exhibited sense of humor. If the lyrics seem awash in cinematic images, that could be because Paul wrote it for *The Graduate*, though it didn't make it into the film. But it did provide some welcome comic relief alongside the more serious moods and subject matter of *Bookends*. And the production elements matched the levity and imagery of the song—a rinky-dink child's piano, the sound effect for Old Roger draft dodger stumbling down the basement steps. There was great imagery throughout: a Kellogg's cornflake floating in a cereal bowl shooting a movie, an English muffin easing its way into the toaster; I wonder how many listeners became "Citizens for Boysenberry Jam" fans after the album was released?

"Punky's Dilemma" is also the last song on *Bookends* for which John Simon receives production-assistance credit. The other production-assistance credits go to Bob Johnston, a Columbia staff producer who had worked successfully with Bob Dylan and Johnny Cash, among others. He is credited as the producer of both *The Sounds of*

Silence album and *Parsley, Sage, Rosemary and Thyme* (though Garfunkel asserts that this was more a matter of music-business politics than hands-on producing. Nonetheless, he is given production-assistance credit on both "A Hazy Shade of Winter" and "At the Zoo" on *Bookends*). When Johnston was asked by *Mix* magazine to contrast his experiences working with Bob Dylan and Simon and Garfunkel, he replied:

> Dylan was fast, and you never knew what he was going to do next. With Paul Simon, something in the studio might take an hour, it might take a day, a week, a month. He was very meticulous. He knew how to make records. He had made lots of demos . . . He really didn't need me or Roy [Halee] except to bounce things off of.

The credits on *Bookends* tell the story in BIG, BOLD LETTERS:

Produced by PAUL SIMON, ART GARFUNKEL & ROY HALEE

Songs by PAUL SIMON

Engineering: ROY HALEE

Halee, of course, had engineered Art and Paul's very first audition session for Columbia, and then all their recordings as a duo. Whatever contributions John Simon or Bob Johnston made, it is clear that by the time *Bookends* was well underway, Simon and Garfunkel had the clout and the talent to take the reins of their own destiny, and they brought Roy Halee along for the ride. Garfunkel described the three-way partnership when he was a guest on the nationally syndicated radio program *In the Studio,* hosted by the disc jockey Redbeard:

"Well, Roy is an engineer, consummate engineer with Rolls Royce standards, and as you know standards are everything. Those who hold to perfectionism knowing that you can get away with much less but you just can't do it because something inside of you says excellence for its own sake—these are the blessed people for me, and Roy is chief amongst this type. And Roy was this wonderful presence, a little older than us, a little more serious, a kind of family man and very lovable. The fact that he was so damned likeable is an important factor, and he was in charge of sounds, and Paul and I got to use him almost like a big-brother figure; we would pitch our ideas to him, and he would be this physiological person that we chose to please with our creativity . . . Roy was a wonderful engineer who thought of sounds the moment he began to hear the songs, and in a sense thereby became coproducer because he did more than just make clean recordings, he made creative sound collages, and I think of him as the third member of our triumph [*sic*]."

Roy confirmed in a 2001 interview with *Mix* magazine

that the nature of his work with Simon and Garfunkel had evolved: "The engineer was the engineer; the producer was the producer. The producer called the shots in the studio. He was running the session, and the engineer followed along. He was considered a good engineer if he didn't get in the way. I was fortunate in that they drew me in more musically; they picked my brain more—'What do you think? What kind of sound would go well with that? What texture might go well with that?' 'Well, how about a piccolo trumpet and a tuba in a church on that?'"

———

There are five songs on side two of *Bookends*. Smack in the middle is the final version of "Mrs. Robinson." Between the time when work on *The Graduate* ended and *Bookends* was completed, Paul added lyrics and verses to the catchy chorus that had been used in the film, to flesh out the snippets that appeared on the soundtrack album. The result was another triumph, their second number-one single and some of the most memorable lyrics Paul Simon has ever written. There were a few reasons for its success.

First of all was its association with the highest-grossing film of 1968—*The Graduate*. The chorus was already known from the movie, so a mass audience was predisposed to hearing the rest of the story.

Once the idea for having the song be about Mrs. Roosevelt was abandoned, Paul obviously tailored the song to the character in the movie and made some very trenchant and witty observations about Mrs. Robinson and about the radically transforming values of younger and older Americans in the 1960s.

Paul thinks there is still some confusion about "Mrs. Robinson": "Now, probably a lot of people don't remember this; they think of the song, they think of the record, but the record wasn't in the movie. The song wasn't even finished when it was in the movie. All we had was the chorus and we sang it with just the guitar. We cut the record after the movie was finished [on February 2, 1968]."

The use of the name *Jesus* in a pop song (in a manner that was not hymnlike or reverent) offended some, but it was also an attention getter, and it had a cachet that set the song apart and made it stand out from other pop songs of the era. Remember how much trouble was stirred up by John Lennon's comment about Jesus in 1966? Oh, and let's not forget Simon and Garfunkel's sly nod to the Beatles' "I Am the Walrus" with the phrase "Coo coo cachoo, Mrs. Robinson."

And perhaps more than anything else, at a time in history when America was mourning slain heroes and looking for someone or something to believe in, Paul struck a nerve and a responsive chord with the question "Where have you gone, Joe DiMaggio?" He told Paul Zollo in *Songwriters on Songwriting*: "The Joe DiMaggio line was written right away in the beginning. And I don't know why or where it came from. It seemed so strange, like it didn't belong in that song, and then, I don't know, it was so interesting to us that we just kept it in. So it's one of the most well-known lines that I've ever written."

There were reports in the newspaper at the time that DiMaggio was unhappy with the reference and even thought about suing over it. Simon, a lifelong New York Yankees fan, dismisses the speculation with his description of their face-to-face meeting. "I saw him in a restaurant one night, and I went over and I said, I'm Paul Simon and I wrote 'Mrs. Robinson.' Oh, he was very polite, you know. He's always said in interviews that he's very flattered by it, but he doesn't have any idea what it means. And then one day, I was talking to Chuck Grodin, who is a friend of mine, and he said, 'Did it ever occur to you that maybe in Joe DiMaggio's mind he didn't think he had gone anywhere? And you say, "Where have you gone, Joe Dimaggio?" He was probably thinking, What do they mean where have I gone? I'm here. I'm living. I'm making commercials. I'm doing my life. Why is he saying where have I gone?' I said, 'Oh no. I never did think of that!'"

When DiMaggio died in 1999, Paul wrote an op-ed piece for the *New York Times* in which he revisited his thoughts about the man and the song:

> The fact that the lines were sincere and that they've been embraced over the years as a yearning for heroes and heroism speaks to the subconscious

desires of the culture. We need heroes and we search for candidates to be anointed . . .

When the hero becomes larger than life, life itself is magnified, and we read with a new clarity our moral compass. The hero allows us to measure ourselves on the goodness scale . . .

In these days of Presidential transgressions and apologies and prime-time interviews about private sexual matters, we grieve for Joe DiMaggio and mourn the loss of his grace and dignity, his fierce sense of privacy, his fidelity to the memory of his wife, and the power of his silence.

———

Tracks four and five on side two of *Bookends* are the other two chart singles that had not yet appeared in album form. And they are also the ones that had production assistance credited to Bob Johnston. "A Hazy Shade of Winter" was an interesting contrast with the first hit single by the Mamas and the Papas, "California Dreaming." John Phillips paints a colorful, romanticized picture of the Golden State, whereas Paul stays true to his dyed-in-the-wool New Yorker status with his stark East Coast winter imagery as yet another metaphor for the passage of time and unfulfilled dreams. And if anyone had the idea that Simon and Garfunkel were just two folkie, sweet-singing troubadours, "Hazy Shade" challenged that assumption. This track rocks!

In 1987, the rocking female group the Bangles, working with famed producer Rick Rubin, did a remake that they called "Hazy Shade of Winter," minus the "A," for the soundtrack of the film *Less Than Zero*. It became a smash hit, reaching number two on the national charts, 11 positions higher than Simon and Garfunkel's original. In addition to the dropped letter in the title, the group also omitted the line referring to "unpublished rhyme." There is a tale told on the Internet that the group sent Paul a basket of limes and a bottle of vodka to make up for the missing lyric. It might not be true, but wouldn't it be great if it were?

"At the Zoo" was another Simon and Garfunkel single that finally made an appearance on this album. Paul's fertile imagination for clever lyrics was in top form. He has an amazing knack for writing songs and melodies that appeal simultaneously to children and adults but for very different reasons. Take, for example, his 1976 number-one single, "50 Ways to Leave Your Lover." Kids love the unending stream of easy names and fun rhymes, and adults nod knowingly about his sly commentary on relationships.

The same is true of "At the Zoo." Children love the

cartoonish animal imagery, and adults snicker at the sometimes witty, sometimes snide anthropomorphizing of the zoo inhabitants:

Monkeys? Honesty! Check.

Giraffes? Insincere! Check.

Pigeons? Secretive! Check.

Hamsters? Well, you don't want to know about the hamsters. And you certainly don't want to know about the zookeeper himself, either!

The last two characterizations are the ones that got Simon in trouble with some zoos, some parents, and some book publishers. Columbia wanted to promote the single at zoos, but was turned down because zoo officials thought the song was insulting to animals. Parents objected to the zookeeper's alleged fondness for rum and the hamsters' presumed propensity for "turning on frequently." Book publishers had the same problem with these characterizations. But in its August 10, 1991, edition, the *New York Times* printed this item:

Paul Simon, pop singer, is now Paul Simon, children's book writer. His first book, *At the Zoo*, is to be published by Doubleday to coincide with his free Central Park concert on Thursday. The Central Park Zoo inspired the book, which is based on Mr.

Simon's hit song of the same title. Valerie Michaut, a leading French illustrator, has filled the pages with zebras in police uniforms, giraffes sporting sunglasses and cheery New York City scenes.

How did these conflicts get resolved? Simple—Simon altered the words in the book to make it more appropriate for children. Instead of liquor, as it is in the song, "Rum" is the name of a beaver that the zookeeper is very fond of! And the hamsters are given headlights that they can "turn on frequently." Brilliant! Parents were happy, the publisher was happy, *and* the world-famous Bronx Zoo ultimately did use the song in one of its radio and television advertising campaigns.

Happy endings all the way around, including for the *Bookends* album itself.

8

POST-*GRADUATE*

Some people will tell you that Simon and Garfunkel's *next* album, *Bridge over Troubled Water*, was the apex of their output as a duo. And yes, commercially it was more successful than anything else they had done, and it won more Grammys, etc. But it's still more a documentation of a partnership being shredded rather than pulled together. There are songs on that album in which you can almost hear Paul thinking about a solo career ("So Long, Frank Lloyd Wright") and others in which Art's contribution is barely audible, as if he had phoned it in from the set of *Catch-22* ("The Only Living Boy in New York"). *Bookends*, on the other hand, showcased Art and Paul as they flexed their musical muscles, taking no prisoners and accomplishing things that even Tom and Jerry could not have imagined in their wildest dreams.

The synergy of *Bookends* and *The Graduate* catapulted them to a level of fame, respect, and popularity that was measurable in any number of ways: First of all, the finished version of "Mrs. Robinson" won the Record of the Year Grammy at the March 1969 awards ceremony. "Mrs. Robinson" also won a Grammy in the Best Contemporary Pop Performance by a Vocal Group or Duo category. And Paul picked up an additional statuette with Dave Grusin as the composers of the Best Original Score for a Motion Picture.

Only a handful of artists have ever had successive number-one albums on the national popularity charts. Simon and Garfunkel did it three times in 1968: *Bookends* replaced *The Graduate* on May 25, *The Graduate* replaced *Bookends* on June 15, and *Bookends* leapfrogged over *The Graduate* again on June 29.

Finally, at one point in 1968, Art and Paul held down *the top three* positions on the national album charts with *Bookends*, the *Graduate* soundtrack, and *Parsley, Sage, Rosemary and Thyme*, which reappeared on the surveys thanks to the legions of new fans who were discovering their music. This was an accomplishment of Beatles-esque proportions that had never happened before and hasn't been matched since.

The added ingredient in their new success was a powerful communications medium exposing their material to a new and bigger audience. Art agreed, "Yes. You bring in all those moms and dads who go to films and you get a whole other thing. 'Mrs. Robinson' became a hit around that time, and I remember it was bringing in another kind of audience. From then on, I would come home from

Europe and the customs guys in New York, the police and the New York customs guys would go, 'Hey, "Mrs. Robinson"!' and I could feel that these guys have just checked in on us."

They rode the crest of this wave for the rest of 1968 and right into 1969. Concert venues got bigger. Album sales continued to soar. And work began on the follow-up project. If it seems that it took the duo an inordinate amount of time to deliver *Bookends*, consider this: The whole of 1969 passed once again without a new album from Simon and Garfunkel. In addition, the only single they released that year was a song recorded on November 16, 1968, that ultimately appeared on the *Bridge* album. It was called "The Boxer," and it climbed to number seven on the charts in the spring of 1969.

One big difference between the long wait for *Bookends* after *Parsley, Sage* and the long wait for *Bridge* after *Bookends* is that this time, the record company laid back. No pressure for new product was exerted, no fatherly talks with Clive Davis were arranged, and no outside producer herded them into the studio to move along that next project. Simon and Garfunkel had become Columbia's 800-pound gorillas who could sit anywhere they wanted to.

After years of indentured servitude to draconian record-company contracts requiring two or even three new albums a year, the most successful and creative recording artists were given some room to breathe and a chance to stretch out and participate in designing the arc of their own careers. Paul assessed the way his albums evolved in this way: "I was thinking the other day that I've made four albums that are very—there's a completeness about them. They are *Bridge over Troubled Water*, *There Goes Rhymin' Simon*, *Still Crazy After All These Years*, and *Graceland*. Then very close, probably right behind, is *Bookends*. The others have good songs and things, but they have too many mistakes. *Mistakes* is the wrong word. They have ideas that aren't fully realized. You usually find whatever the idea is on the next album. I figure it out and do it right. What happens is that the album that precedes these has the seeds for the album that follows. *Bridge over Troubled Water* takes what was good about *Bookends*, keeps it, and discards the other stuff."

The song "Bridge over Troubled Water" is the quintessential Art Garfunkel vocal performance. Even though Paul wrote it, many consider it to be more Art's song than his, including Paul. "It's just like a song that I wrote," Paul said, "but in some ways I can't even remember that I wrote it or how I wrote it. I guess that's partly because Artie sang most of it. I only joined in on the last verse, but, I mean, it was this enormous hit—such a big hit all around the world. It just sort of leaves you and becomes something else, somebody else's thing."

Art cut to the chase: "It's a great song. It's one of Paul's great achievements in writing. It's a vocal I'm very proud of. It cost me a lot of sweat to get it. I did many retakes. I remember getting the last verse first and soaring away on the high notes in a most euphorically happy way. I remember the second verse, wanting to get a medium amount of strength, and obviously the build was the thing I was working on. But the first verse took me 'umpteen' recording sessions. I went through hell and back and then more hell and back again . . . I wanted that first verse just the way I wanted it. I knew it had to be cat quiet to set up the second verse, and as I was doing it I began to know just what I was looking for and I sort of couldn't settle for anything less, and just to have the control to execute what you began to hear was not easy."

Based on what had happened with "The Dangling Conversation" in 1966, Art didn't think of "Bridge" as a potential hit. "No," he said. "I thought it was clearly an album cut, definitely never a single, and I thought it was a strong album cut. Good song. Good vocal. Like 'Hey Jude,' one of those bigger records. I was pleased with it, but I must say it was received better than I thought [it would be]. It was a single and a big hit single—thanks to [Columbia's president at the time] Clive Davis's confidence that it could be. And it just went down bigger than I thought."

When asked what chords he thought it tapped into among the record-buying public, Art replied, "Maybe one of the ingredients is how universal the sentiment of the lyric is that Paul wrote. When you're in trouble, I will lay down for you. It is Christ's message. It's every loyal friend. Call me when you need me, I will always be there for you. Now there is something we love to believe—that humans give each other that dependable support when it's needed. We love to feel that that can be counted on."

Everyone knows about what went right with *Bridge*. Art Garfunkel weighed in on what went wrong with it: "The funny thing about that album is that we weren't getting along very well in those days. We had just been with each other for too many tours and concerts and albums—too much pressure to keep it going. So as that album was progressing, I think both of us were thinking, 'It's turning out well, but it ain't that much fun.' It's odd that things that are sometimes difficult lead to good results. I'm very proud of *Bridge over Troubled Water*. The album has got good variety in it. If you can open an album with the long, big ballad, 'Bridge over Troubled Water,' and then go to 'I'd rather be a sparrow than a snail' ['El Condor Pasa'] and have all that Peruvian sound, and then go to 'Cecilia,' you're having the fun of showing off in all these different directions, which makes for variety."

One of the most famous stories about dissension between Simon and Garfunkel during the recording sessions for *Bridge* involves the phantom 12th song. Just like *Parsley, Sage, Rosemary and Thyme* and *Bookends*, *Bridge over Troubled Water* was supposed to contain the then fairly standard dozen tracks. There are only 11. Why? Because Art and Paul were deadlocked over the choice of a 12th selection. Paul had written an obviously political song called "Cuba Sí, Nixon No" that Artie refused to record. And Paul put the kibosh on a Bach chorale that Artie wanted to put on the album. The "old friends" dug in. No compromise, no negotiation, no meeting halfway; the album was released with just 11 songs.

When asked if he ever speculated about what might have happened if the duo had stayed together, Art paused momentarily and began answering the question by speaking about Simon and Garfunkel in the third person: "I like those guys. They were a great duo. I wish they could have made more albums, and if they ever do make another album, I suspect they will pick up where they left off and make a good one. They are not arrested talents, neither of them, those two guys, Paul and Artie. They are committed to growing at what they do and they would probably combine very interestingly musically if they ever did combine again. But they are just a fiction now. They are on the shelf. They are in our imaginations. I have a lot of affection for them and miss them. But that's academic, you know. I'm kind of hung up with that feeling, along with many fans, so I may as well not frustrate me or the fans and talk about it because what can you do?"

Art conceded that "The Only Living Boy in New York" and "So Long, Frank Lloyd Wright" are about him. About the latter, he revealed, "Paul says he wrote that with me in mind because I was an architecture student at Columbia in the early sixties, and this was his way of saying, 'Artie, whether you realize it or not, I'm checking out when this is over. So long!'" he laughed. "But I think both of us were feeling that when this album is over, we'll both need a little rest for a while. I don't hate you, but at the moment I do." Of course, it went on to be this phenomenal, almost uncontrollable success. "It was the biggest album of all albums to that point. It sold more than anything else. What can you say? We were determined to move on and take a rest from each other no matter what it did. So it almost looks like we did that hip thing of leaving at the height of our success. But the fact that it was so successful came after the split, if you want to call it that. I never thought of it as a split. I just thought of it as 'I'll see you later, but maybe not for a few months.'"

Those few months turned into decades. The mists of time have blurred how quickly we discovered that, when it came to Simon and Garfunkel, the whole was greater than the sum of its parts. Yes, both have had stunning solo successes, but nothing stirs the imagination or brings fans old and new out of the woodwork faster than even the faintest possibility of a Simon and Garfunkel reunion. So what explains the hold the duo has on an audience, and a generation for that matter, that the individuals do not? Art said that "as a member of this former duo, that question is wonderfully rich and deep, I think. It is about duality to me. It is that two elements—each themselves and the sum total, and the air between them, and the touching of the membrane that separates them—there's a lot that goes on in duality and in how the mind perceives any two things. Where there is a complementary two, there is great entertainment in that packaging. Now I was one of the two, and I was very involved in projecting that duality in as interesting a way as I could. Maybe instinctively from the moment I teamed up with Paul, I felt I'm blond, he's dark; I'm taller, he's shorter. There's already a different but interesting, complementary thing going on here. How do I instinctively make the most of that? Well, maybe instinctively we both did that well and, more than I can even analyze, the public bought it."

Of course, they have gotten back together on numerous occasions along the way. Simon and Garfunkel reunited as early as 1972 to perform at a rally for Democratic presidential nominee George McGovern at Madison Square Garden in New York. It was a clever idea. Three groups that were not performing together at that time reunited to support their candidate: Mike Nichols and Elaine May; Peter, Paul and Mary; and Simon and Garfunkel. Other reunions have also taken place at various times for various reasons (induction into the Rock and Roll Hall of Fame in 1990, accepting the Grammy Lifetime Achievement Award in 2003, touring, a month of concerts in New York City at a performance hall at Madison Square Garden in 1993), but true to form, there have also been long periods when the "old friends" weren't even speaking to one another. Hands down, the most spectacular reunion of all was the free concert that the boys did in New York's Central Park on September 19, 1981, when 500,000 fans swarmed into the park on a damp, cloudy Saturday afternoon and into the evening to hear and cheer their heroes.

Art recalled that evening of the concert in Central Park in this way: "These are the days in the early eighties when it was tough to get a picture of Paul and Artie together that they both approved of," he laughed. Both artists agree that the choice of material on the double-album recording of the performance, *The Concert in Central Park*, is a good representation of who and what Simon and Garfunkel were all about. The tunes were carefully chosen, as they were for all their collaborations, and there were also a few tantalizing glimpses of what some Paul Simon solo songs might have sounded like if they had been Simon and Garfunkel songs instead ("Late in the Evening," "Slip Slidin' Away," etc.). When asked if performing on Paul's solo work was easy for him to do, Art replied with a smile, "Musically it was pretty easy for most of them. Psychologically, it was a little tricky because it made me want to say, 'I've had hits in my solo career. Where's Paul harmonizing on my tunes?' But . . . ooops! . . . I didn't say that!" he laughed.

Most of the disagreements between Art and Paul

seemed to result from some kind of artistic tension. Art confirmed this. "That's pretty much what it is," he said. "All the fights we had, had to do with 'We want to give the public the most value for their money,' so they're all about 'Put the accordion in the second verse, not the last verse.' It's all that kind of stuff. Your tension comes out of your desire to serve the public to the max." In the *Concert* album packaging, there is a photo, shot from behind the duo, that shows them with their arms around each other, acknowledging the cheers of the crowd. "It's an honest photo," Art said. "There we are kind of hugging each other like the friends we are. Yeah, that's good. You can't leave that stuff out if it's true."

Paul recalled the concert in this way: "The reunion? That night was a night that I'll never forget. It still has the same glow to me. It was a total surprise to us. We thought, of course, that a lot of people would come, but we had no idea that it was going to be a half a million people. I said, let's tape it, let's just have it. We didn't expect to put a record out from it. We didn't expect anything other than that night. There isn't really a visual record of Simon and Garfunkel. Very little."

When he was shown the picture from the album package of him and Art hugging and asked whether the undercurrent of their reunion represented something even bigger to their fans, Paul replied, "That's right, about the possibility of reunion, that's right. It symbolically said wounds can be healed, things can go back to the way they were. Life has a happy ending—all those things that we desperately wish to be true. And which sometimes are true. Mostly they're not, but they can be true. And the soul's desire to have them be true is so strong that when something symbolizes it, it just floods our emotions. That may be it."

It isn't that that "may be it," it's that that is it *exactly*!

PS

As long as they continue to walk this earth and choose to perform, alone or together, Paul Simon and Art Garfunkel will attract the attention of music lovers all around the globe. Of course, the future is unknowable, the judgment of history an everchanging conundrum subject to reinterpretation and revision. But that has never stopped the critics, pundits, historians, musicians, and fans alike from offering their "irrefutable" and "unimpeachable" opinions about events that have not yet taken place. Here's mine: In a world where most of the output of popular culture is ephemeral and disposable, a world in which we are drowning in a tsunami of the trivial and prurient, the music of Simon and Garfunkel will last. It will continue to attract audiences and interest long after all of us who are conscious right now are dust.

Paul Simon will maintain his status as a preeminent songwriter and performer, *but* his solo accomplishments will always take a backseat to the Simon and Garfunkel legacy. As we go to press, his most recent honor is the first-ever Library of Congress Gershwin Prize for Popular Song, which was presented during a ceremony in the library's Great Hall on May 23, 2007. An all-star lineup (including James Taylor, Stevie Wonder, and Ladysmith Black Mambazo) paid tribute to Paul by performing songs from his bountiful catalog. But the moment that electrified the crowd, the moment that most will remember, is when Paul stepped up to the microphone and said, "I'd like to introduce my dear friend and partner in arguments . . ." It was, of course, Artie Garfunkel who brought down the house with yet another performance of "Bridge over Troubled Water."

As I said earlier, when it comes to Simon and Garfunkel, the whole will always be greater than the sum of its parts. In a discussion about some of the many honors they have received, I once asked Paul about entering the Rock and Roll Hall of Fame in 1990. Employing his trademark understated sense of humor, he answered, "Very unlikely that I'll get into the Hall of Fame, although I did have a couple of good years as a pitcher." When I pressed him about it, he relented, "That's a nice honor—the Rock and Roll Hall of Fame. It has all the people that you idolized as a kid in there, so it becomes an honor to join them. Of course, the thought that I had in my head was when Artie and I were kids pretending that we were disc jockeys and putting on rock-and-roll records and imitating rock-and-roll artists. We never could possibly imagine that we would be included in the same group as Fats Domino and Chuck Berry and Sam Cooke and Elvis Presley and the Everly Brothers, particularly the Everly Brothers." (In one of the more heartwarming gestures in rock'n'roll history, Simon and Garfunkel did a very classy thing when they successfully reunited and went on tour in 2003. They brought the Everlys along with them *not* as an opening act, but rather as midconcert special guests performing their signature hits "Bye, Bye Love," "Wake Up Little Susie," and "All I Have to Do Is Dream." It served as a way of focusing attention on Don and Phil and showcasing them to an audience that might not have experienced their greatness firsthand.)

Another Hall of Fame has beckoned the duo to join its ranks, and this one is much closer to home, literally and figuratively. The Long Island Music Hall of Fame has inducted Simon and Garfunkel into its Class of 2007, and a certain New York radio personality who has loved and played their music on the radio for more than 40 years has been asked to do the honors on October 21, 2007. (That would be me!)

As we wind down this examination of "Bookends," truly one of their greatest accomplishments, I'm going to close with Art Garfunkel's passionate, unspoiled response to my question about whether the awards mean anything to them and whether they draw on that tremendous reservoir of good feeling that they have put out into the world. He answered emphatically, "Absolutely yes! Now you're talking about perhaps the sweetest part of my life. People in the streets who give me this feeling of 'I really, really love what you're doing. Keep doing it.' Or, 'You have given me many pleasurable moments. Thank you.' When I hear that, I'm so touched, I can't tell you. I have never acquired any jadedness or cynicism to the repetition of that wonderful exchange. When I hear that, I go, 'Well damned if that ain't what I've dedicated my life to!' And there's the completion of that circle. It couldn't be sweeter."

And that's the way the *Bookends* book ends.

SIMON AND GARFUNKEL
SELECTED DISCOGRAPHY

WEDNESDAY MORNING, 3 A.M.

You Can Tell the World

Last Night I Had the Strangest Dream

Bleeker Street

Sparrow

Benedictus

The Sound of Silence (sic)

He Was My Brother

Peggy-O

Go Tell It on the Mountain

The Sun Is Burning

The Times They Are A-Changin'

Wednesday Morning, 3 A.M.

Produced by Tom Wilson

SOUNDS OF SILENCE (sic)

The Sound of Silence (sic)
Leaves That Are Green
Blessed
Kathy's Song
Somewhere They Can't Find Me
Anji
Richard Cory
A Most Peculiar Man
April Come She Will
We've Got a Groovy Thing Going
I Am a Rock

Produced by Bob Johnston

PARSLEY, SAGE, ROSEMARY AND THYME

Scarborough Fair/Canticle
Patterns
Cloudy
Homeward Bound
The Big Bright Green Pleasure Machine
The 59th Street Bridge Song (Feelin' Groovy)
The Dangling Conversation
Flowers Never Bend with the Rainfall
A Simple Desultory Phillipic
(Or How I Was Robert McNamara'd into Submission)
For Emily, Whenever I May Find Her
A Poem on the Underground Wall
7 O'Clock News/Silent Night

Produced by Bob Johnston

BOOKENDS

Bookends Theme
Save the Life of My Child*
America
Overs*
Voices of Old People
Old Friends
Bookends Theme
Fakin' It*
Punky's Dilemma*
Mrs. Robinson (From the motion picture "The
　　Graduate")
A Hazy Shade of Winter**
At the Zoo**

Produced by Paul Simon, Art Garfunkel, and Roy Halee
Songs by Paul Simon
Engineer: Roy Halee
*Production Assistance: John Simon
**Production Assistance: Bob Johnston
Arrangement of "Old Friends": Jimmy Haskell

BRIDGE OVER TROUBLED WATER

Bridge over Troubled Water
El Condor Pasa (If I Could)
Cecilia
Keep the Customer Satisfied
So Long, Frank Lloyd Wright
The Boxer
Baby Driver
The Only Living Boy in New York
Why Don't You Write Me
Bye Bye Love
Song for the Asking

Produced by Paul Simon, Arthur Garfunkel, and Roy Halee
Engineer: Roy Halee
Recordist: Ted Brosnan

RESOURCES

Unless otherwise noted directly in the text, all of the first-person quotes from Simon and Garfunkel in this manuscript were culled from my personal archive of interviews with Paul and Art, which began when we first met after a concert at Fordham University in December of 1966, and continued over time into the twenty-first century!

Other valuable resources included the following:

Aames, Morgan. "Simon and Garfunkel in Action." *High Fidelity*, November 1967, 62.

Bronson, Fred. *The Billboard Book of Number One Hits*. New York: Billboard Books, 1985.

Douglas, Susan J. *Listening In: Radio and American Imagination*. New York: Times Books, 1999.

Flanagan, Bill. *Written in My Soul*. Chicago: Contemporary Books, 1986.

Fornatale, Peter. *The Story of Rock 'n' Roll*. New York: William Morrow and Company, 1987.

Fornatale, Peter, and Joshua E Mills. *Radio in the Television Age*. Woodstock, NY: The Overlook Press, 1980.

Fricke, David. *Old Friends,* liner notes. New York: Columbia/ Legacy Records, 1997.

Hoskyns, Barney. *Led Zeppelin IV*. Emmaus: Rodale, 2006.

Johnson, Pete. "Simon and Garfunkel: The Despair and Hope of Loneliness." *Hit Parader*, November 1968, 9.

Marcus, Greil, ed. *Rock and Roll Will Stand*. Boston: Beacon Press, 1969.

Marmorstein, Gary. *The Label: The Story of Columbia Records*. New York: Thunder's Mouth Press, 2007.

Reid, Jan. *Layla and Other Assorted Love Songs by Derek and the Dominos*. Emmaus: Rodale, 2006.

Taylor, Derek. *It Was Twenty Years Ago Today*. New York: Fireside, 1987.

Whitburn, Joel. *The Billboard Book of Top 40 Hits*. New York: Billboard Books, 1983.

Zollo, Paul. *Songwriters on Songwriting*. Cambridge, MA: Da Capo Press, 2003.

ACKNOWLEDGMENTS

After 40-plus years on the radio, I am well aware of the vast differences between the spoken word and the printed word. The former is a somewhat ephemeral experience.

You say the words. They either hit or miss their intended target, and then they just evaporate into thin air or (nowadays) drift off into cyberspace.

Writing a book is a whole other matter. There's a much greater sense that the words will survive you. They are more carefully chosen and chiseled than the ones ad-libbed or spoken extemporaneously. I am still stunned, then gratified, when I walk into a library or bookstore and find one of my earlier publications on the shelves. It is an incomparable thrill. So my first thank-you on this page is to the man who launched my second career as an author more than 25 years ago and is still a valued and trusted friend—Mark Gompertz.

I've been blessed with terrific writing partners and collaborators all along the way and would like to single out the following for making me a better writer, a better friend, and, hopefully, a better person: Bill Ayres, Nancy Bailey, Matt Billy, Marty Brooks, David Buskin, Becky

Cabaza, Nancy Elgin, Dennis Elsas, Nikki Esposito, Linda Feder, Jerry Garfunkel, Kevin Goldman, Julian Gompertz, Paul Graham, Chris Hall, Wayne Kabak, Alan Katz, Bill Kollar, Paul Kurland, Steve Leeds, Arthur Levy, Mike Marrone, Steve Matteo, Don McGee, Roger McGuinn, the late Hank Medress, Ed Micone, Fred Migliore, Josh Mills, Marilyn Munder, Graham Nash, Cathy Petrone, Chip Rachlin, Michael Reinert, the late Steve Sawyer, Don Thiergard, and Glenn Zagoren. Special thanks to Dr. Steve Greenberg and Dr. Judy Marcus.

For this project, I add a new name to the list: Peter Thomas Fornatale. A talented writer and packager in his own right, he is also a superb editor who seems to effortlessly yet firmly get the absolute best out of his authors. The fact that his father is one of those authors makes this accomplishment even more impressive. There were no troubled waters, no sounds of silence, no dangling conversations. I won't overdo the imagery by claiming that we were feelin' groovy all the time, but I will say that the existence of this book is further proof that the Child is Father to the Man. (Thank you, Gerard Manley Hopkins and Al Kooper.)

As for the bookends that hold this manuscript together, let me start by thanking each of them for the music that has been so important and special to me and to millions of others for more than 40 years now. And also let me thank them for the quality time that we spent together over those years (without handler interference!), getting to know one another and delving deeply into all aspects of the personal and professional wellspring that is Simon and Garfunkel.

I would also like to offer special thanks to the legendary record producer and performer John Simon for sharing his time, his knowledge, his stories, and his great sense of humor with me. I know that his participation has made this a better book.

My friend Chip Rachlin says that a baseball game looks different to you when you get to the later innings. I think the same is true of life. It has been a privilege for me to document the album that now spans the lifetime of a generation. In this troubled and divided world, perhaps there is still one thing we can all agree on: Preserve your memories; they're all that's left you.

Now where have I heard that before?

ACKNOWLEDGMENTS